CONTENTS

100 Years

Kinmel Camp

Written by John D. Johnson

First published in 2019

Bowmanvillejohn@hotmail.com

ISBN 978-1543163572

Published by

CreateSpace

Endorsements

Colonel Howard G Coombs OMM,CD, Ph.D.
Canadian Armed Forces, Kingston, Ontario

John D Johnson's "100 Years Kinmel Camp" puts together the perspectives of various military personnel and groups that served at Kinmel Camp over the past century. While not an in-depth history of the camp during the period it provides much human detail for both the amateur and professional historian alike. It gives a start point for further research concerning various aspects of the British and Canadian experience at Kinmel, as well as the military history of the region. Mr. Johnson is to be commended on his passion that he has brought to this topic and the hard work evidenced in putting together this collection of experiences.

Howard

Major Floyd Low CD (retired)
Canadian Royal Engineers

John Johnson has traced a military family link back to Kinmel Park Camp and those of many Welshmen who passed through its gates, cutting through 100 years of dusty forgotten files and newspapers to bring out a very readable popular history of the men and women who stood up for King and Country so long ago. In doing so John has blazed a trail for future study. "Well Done That Man".

Floyd

Captain Dale Gray CD (Retired)
The Ontario Regiment (Royal Canadian Armoured Corps)

I found John's book on Kinmel Park Camp extremely well written and researched. As an armchair historian of the Canadian Expeditionary Force, this is a story that all Canadians need to know, from the Royal Canadian Medical Services of those men and women that gave their lives in caring for wounded and sick patients, to the men of the Reserve Battalions and Serving Forces waiting in Kinmel Park Camp to go home, which for some, had been years of service at the front only to be put in a camp that was overcrowded, with men sleeping on the bare floor of their barrack rooms, with the threat of dying of influenza. (The Spanish Flu)

A fantastic read for any Canadian and those from Britain to a little known story of Service and Sacrifice.

Dale

Chronology of Events at Kinmel Park Camp

4th August 1914
War is declared between Great Britain and Germany.

February 1915
The railway Line is completed to Kinmel Park Camp.

7th August 1917
The War Department take over responsibility for the Railway on KPC.

March 1915
The first of 15000 soldiers start arriving.

26th November 1915
Lord Harlech the Colonel of the newly formed Welsh Guards visits Kinmel Camp, recruiting for the Guards.

June 1916
40000 soldiers are encamped at KPC

20th August 1916
The Right Honourable David Lloyd George visits the KPC.

7th January 1919
Men of No2 Construction Company were involved in a melee.

5th/6th March 1919
The Canadian soldier's riot at Kinmel Park Camp.

1920's
Kinmel Park Camp was used as an internment camp.

May 1933
The Kings Own Royal Regiment have their annual Camp at Kin-

mel Park Camp.

3rd September 1939

War declared on Germany by Great Britain.

1939/45

News Black Out for the duration of the WW2.

4th May 1945

Peace declared in Europe.

15th August 1945

Victory over Japan.

June 1950

Korean War commences.

1953

The 38th Training Regiment Royal Artillery take over Kinmel Camp.

July 1954

Korean War (Armistice)

1962

The Junior Leaders Training Regiment take over Kinmel Camp.

1974

The Junior Leaders Training Regiment are disbanded.

1980

The Territorial Army take over Kinmel Camp.

1994

Police Helicopter Flight base their flight at Kinmel Camp.

1999
The NW Police Flight Leaves Kinmel Camp. **2000**
The Territorial's hand Kinmel Camp over to the Army Cadet Force.

2014
The Military Training Awareness Team take
over Kinmel.

Mr John D Johnson

Photographs

1. A view of Kinmel Camp
2. Members of the 12th Reserve Battalion RWF
3. The Royal Welsh parading on Rhyl Promenade
4. F Company lines No 20 Camp
5. RMS/SS Olympic
6. Bdr Thomas Cains – RFA - CEF
7. Lcpl Ivor Morgan - SWB
8. Postcard written by Lcpl Ivor Morgan
9. YMCA letter written by Lcpl Ivor Morgan
10. Salvation Army letter written by Pte Ivor Morgan
11. Letter written by Pre Ivor Morgan
12. Medals of Lt.Col T.J Terrell - Royal Horse Artillery
13. Pte John (Jack) Babcock – 146th Battalion – CEF
14. John Johnson (the Author) with his memorial in Bowmanville, The Royal Canadian Legion
15. Bolton and Farnworth boys at Kinmel Park Camp
16. Pte Jack Bowden – Welsh Regiment
17. Men of the Welsh Regiment
18. Men of the RWF Pte Richard Williams (marked by a cross)
19. Postcard - Canada for Ever
20. Postcard 4th Division CEF
21. Post Card - I am proud of you my boy
22. Postcard The Call of the Flag
23. St. Thomas Church Rhyl
24. Morfa Hall Rhyl
25. Conscientious Objector (Satire)
26. Harding Rees
27. Pte Worsley and friends RWF
28. Lord French visits KPC
29. 12th Battalion the Welsh Regiment under canvas
30. Pte Francis Thomas RWF
31. Pte William Benjamin Johnstone
32. Newspaper clipping four son's in five years
33. The Hospital Ship St. Andrews

34.   Military Medal citation for Lcpl Frank Thorley
35.   Cap Badge 2rd Construction Battalion CEF
36.   Members of a Construction Battalion CEF
37.   Capture of Lt. Cmdr H Tholens (German Navy)
38.   38th Brigade (The Welsh Division) Monument at Memetz Wood
39.   Death Penny of Pte Fred Rowlands
40.   Last Bus from Kinmel Park
41.   St. Margaret's Church Yard, Bodelwyddan
42.   Members of the Kings Own Royal Regiment 1933
43.   Some Officers at KPC in the 30's
44.   An Artillery Unit under canvas at KPC sometime in also in the 1930's
45.   A Search Light Unit at Kinmel Camp – WW2
46.   81st Training Battery - RA – 1956
47.   3.7 Anti-Aircraft Gun
48.   The Unit Patch
49.   Christmas Card by Gnr G Clayton
50.   Officers Mess Bat Staff
51.   Junior Training Regiment Rhyl unit sign
52.   The Bed Block
53.   Barrack ready for Inspection
54.   Trooper David Jenkins - 1st The Queen's Dragoon Guards
55.   Trooper Stephen Carter - 1st The Queen's Dragoon Guards
56.   An alter in one of the Churches at Kinmel Camp

57.   A "Leave Pass" for a young soldier
58.   Permanent Staff Members AATR
59.   TJTRR Plaque
60.   Young soldiers during a field craft exercise 1971
61.   Diagram of the Kinmel Camp training facility WW1 training trenches
62.   Police Helicopter G-NWPI
63.   Euro Copter EC-135 G-NWPS
64.   Military Training Awareness Course Staff
65.   Lance/Sgt Nuttall – RWF

66.   The Headstone of Pte J. Wood 1st Canadian Mounted Rifles – CEF

67.   The Head Stone of Private William Ryder 53rd Young Soldiers Battalion The Welsh Regiment.

Glossary

A short glossary of abbreviations:

AKA: Also Known As
ATS: Auxiliary Territorial Service
APTC: Army Physical Training Corps
CBE: Companion British Empire
CD: Canadian Decoration
CCAS: Canadian Clearing Aid Station
CEF: Canadian Expeditionary Force
CMC: Canadian Medical Centre
TB: Tuberculosis
CMMC: Canadian Army Medical Corps
VE: Victory in Europe
DSO: Distinguished Service Ord
CCMD: The Most Distinguished Order of St. Michael and St. George
GCM: Good Conduct Medal
HMT: His Majesty's Transport
HAC: Honorable Artillery Company
KCB: Most Honorable Order of the Bath
KPC: Kinmel Park Camp
LMH: Kitchener Military Hospital
MC: Military Cross
MID   Mentioned in Dispatches
MCOS: Military College of Science
NAAFI: Navy Army Air Force Institute
NWCFA: North Wales Coast Football Association
NCO: None Commissioned Officer
OOB: Out of Bounds
PC: Post Card
POW: Prisoner of War
QAIMNS: Queen Alexandria Imperial Nursing Service
RASC: Royal Army Service Corps
RAMTS: Royal Artillery Mechanical Traction

RMS: Royal Mail Ship
SWB: South Wales Borderers
RWF: Royal Welsh Fusiliers
WAAC: Women's Army Auxiliary Corps
Gnr: Gunner
Dvr: Driver
Spr: Sapper
Bn: Battalion

Preface

Above: Kinmel Park Camp (1)

You may wonder what on earth motivated me embark on the challenge of constructing a book of this nature. This is a question I admit I posed to myself often hypothetically throughout this process of seemingly relentless investigation.

Sitting down to articulate an answer to this question served to remind me that I commissioned myself the task of collating the facts of military history with memories and dedications of servicemen of the past to share them with generations of the future.

Several contributing factors inspired me to put pen to paper in memorandum of those whose services I felt should be documented and be remembered, "Lest We Forget". My personal friend Mr. Jerry Bone, a local historian from Prestatyn, prompted me to document the findings of an investigation I had come to undertake through curiosity. I have become a local resident of the area and had discovered there were links with Kinmel Park Camp to my family history. I wanted to find out more.

My Great Grand Father 171637 Lance Corporal William Lees-Johnson of the 3rd Battalion, The Ontario Regiment was stationed at Kinmel Park Camp, whilst convalescing at the end of World War One. He arrived in the United Kingdom on the 'SS Olympic' (SS = Steam Ship) in 1915. He had been wounded in a bomb attack on the regimental headquarters by a German warplane near Arras, France on 15th September 1918. I had found the incident recorded in the Regimental History Book "Battle Royal" (page 253) during research into my family ancestry.

Subsequently my great-grandfather left the United Kingdom on the 4th January 1919, sailing on the 'SS Aquitania' returning to Canada from Liverpool. I strived to find out more about his time in North Wales, a region I'd been living in for some years now. There were no straight forward sources through which to learn more. An additional reason for my motivation was that I found that Kinmel Park Camp is a part of Canada's military history. Canada became my second home, thus, I felt driven to utilize my affiliation with both locations concerned along with my personal interest to bring Kinmel Park Camp to the attention of people both sides of the pond. Whilst residing in North Wales, after retiring from service in 1st The Queens Dragoon Guards I became a Warrant Officer with 856 Chirk Squadron, Air Training Corps. In 1994, I took part in a Remembrance Parade which was held at Kinmel Camp. Our squadron organized the parade which, at that time, was supported by the local community of Bodelwyddan and the surrounding towns and organizations. A large party of Canadians who were visiting from Alberta, Canada, were in attendance, aware of a military connection to the site. I felt disappointed that I could not present our visitors with an awful lot of literature about the military connections we shared when it was requested.

I found since that there have been three books written on Kinmel Camp, "The Story of Kinmel Park Military Training Camp 1914 to 1918" and Riots, Death and Baseball (The Canadians at Kinmel Camp 1918-19) by Robert H. Griffiths two truly great efforts by Robert and the "Kinmel Park Camp Riots 1919" written by Mr. Julian Putkowski.

These books are excellent and well researched. There are also works by Canadians such as Colonel Howard G Coombs, a personal friend of mine. I will be using some of their observations within this book. However, my intension is to cover the ground they hadn't covered in their works but due to the lack of information out there, inevitably there will some sharing of information.

My wife and I immigrated to Canada. However, in 2012, due to a family member's ill-heath, we re-located back to North Wales. My wife Jaci and I settled in a seaside town less than ten miles away from Kinmel Camp, Old Colwyn. My wife and I have been asked by the High Commission of Canada and The Royal Canadian Legion on two separate occasions to lay wreaths at St. Margret's Church (also known as the Marble Church), Bodelwyddan, during their Remembrance Day observances. What a great privilege! During the time we have lived in North Wales I have met numerous people whose kind words of support have encouraged me in this undertaking. To those I am truly thankful. Of note, I would like to highlight that the British Archives in London informed me they have nothing on Kinmel Park Camp, especially for the period 1939-45. Quite amazing in all honesty.

Dedication

I would like to dedicate this work as most military historians seem to do these days, to every "Serviceman or Woman" and Civilian who served at the establishment over the past 100 years, to me there could be no better dedication. Every name I have come across during my research has been included in this book in one way or another. I have strived to include a short story about each of them in recognition of their service.

My Personal Thanks

I wish to express my huge gratitude to Major (retired) Floyd Low, a Sapper of long ago of the Royal Canadian Engineers, who was my aid in Ottawa visiting the Archives of Canada on many occasions on my behalf, also to Mr. Tom Burke a friend and neighbour for designing the cover for this book. Lastly, to Malcomb Pugh for his help in the resizing of the photographs here in. Thank you, gentlemen.

My Sincere thanks to all the resources I have used in my research. They have all have a special mention at the back of this book.

CHAPTER 1

No 4 FIELD MILITIA DEPARTMENT

FIELD ARMY ROYAL ARTILLERY – was the
original name of the camp.

Back Ground History 1914 - 1919 Kinmel Park Camp

The British Government gave an ultimatum to the German Government that if they did not stop their hostilities against neutral Belgium, then a state of war would exist between the two nations. On the 4th August, 1914 war was declared on Germany by the British Government. With that in mind, the War Department set about looking for places to build military establishments for the training of soldiers. The Kinmel Park Estate had been used by the War Department for training purposes during the late 1800's, under tented conditions in support of the Boar War. It was a simple choice to use this estate as the new military training establishment in Wales, at a cost of £350,000, to be built by "McAlpine's". It was to be built on the land procured by the War Department from the Kinmel Park Estate. The Camp was built on lush parkland which, in time, was to become the largest military training establishment in Wales during the Great War. The camp's principle function was to train men to become soldiers ready for active service. In the later years the camp was used for soldiers for convalescence, as well as a detention center for conscientious objectors. It also billeted young soldier battalions especially towards the end of the war. The young soldier battalions had under-age young men within its ranks. They would be trained to the same standard as the regular service men, and be deployed once they reached the age of nineteen years. It is to be noted some young men had been brought back from the front, as they were found to be under age. Some had been given honours for bravery and wore wound strips, plus they held promotions, which did not go down too well with the instructor cadre at Kinmel. Initially, the camp was to billet two thousand British (Welsh) troops. By the end of the First World War, the camp billeted in excess of twenty thousand (Canadian) troops. It should be noted, that after the Canadians left Kinmel Camp twenty thousand Welshmen took their place readying themselves for demobilising. During the 1920's, the camp was used as an internment camp to house Southern Irish political prisoners and as a special hospital for those suffering with VD (Venereal Disease.) The camp covered a most extensive area. It was the biggest military establishment in Wales but it was very basic. Within its confines were a Cinema, NAAFI, YMCA club, and a couple of churches, as well as some civilian shops, which supported the soldiers with certain basic needs. By 1918 it held twenty cantonments (camps) which were made into eleven autonomous wings. These mirrored the military districts of Canada, within its confines. This was initiated during the Canadians short stay. A total of twenty-eight different British Units/Regiments used the camp during the period leading up to 1918.

Above: A photograph of some members of the 12th Reserve Battalion Royal Welsh Fusiliers (2)

Kinmel Camp during the First World War

Having researched this book for over six years, finding short stories of events open to me, chance meetings, old newspaper clippings, books, libraries and the archives at Hawarden, Flintshire. The list goes on and on. It has been for me, a long road. Each story has in my opinion earned its place in the history of Kinmel Park Camp. Three years ago, I found another interesting story, by yet again another chance meeting. I met a chap in Orono, Ontario, Canada, whose Great Grand Father and Great Uncle, the McDonalds, were both members of the Canadian Royal Artillery and were at the camp during the rioting, claiming he had photographs of the event and personal letters written and sent back to their Mother about the event. Sadly, I was not able to get hold of any of these items. Even after visiting the shop on one further occasion. The one that got away, I guess.

The Building of Kinmel Park Camp

The Camp was built on flat, low-lying ground known as the Rhuddlan Marsh, situated on the west side of the River Clwyd estuary. At the time, the construction of a railway link was underway to supply the site initially with building materials. W. Alban Richards & Company, was the main company used during the construction. A total of three standard gauge locomotives were used during the period of construction. They continued work throughout 1915-16, when on 7th August 1916 the War Department took over the railway from the contractor. The War Department used two former locomotives from the Shropshire & Montgomery Railway. They were known as the 'Thisbe' and the 'Pyramus'. The Thisbe was soon returned to Longmoor, in Hampshire (Longmoor is a supply depot still in use to this day). The Thisbe was replaced by the 'Sir John French'. Also used at the Kinmel Park Camp, was the 'Northumbria'. On the 14th June 1917, a line was officially opened between Rhyl and the Camp by Sir Pitcairn Campbell KCB. He was the General Officer Commanding Weston Command at the time. Soldiers used the new line to get into the town of Rhyl, where they frequented the local public houses, cinemas and dance halls. These trains were often full to overflowing, with some servicemen using the carriage roof tops, especially on the last train back to Kinmel Camp. Local Tradesmen, men from the Ministry of Labour's training school, Capel Curig, and local laborers (some five hundred plus men) were eventually employed on the construction, working twelve hour shifts, seven days a week.

General Owen Thomas

Sometime during 1915, General Owen Thomas (soon to become General Sir Owen Thomas) used Kinmel Park Camp as his Headquarters. It was here, he was under the impression he was putting together a Welsh Army. Mr. Lloyd George (Prime Minister) spoke about the Welsh Army wearing its own distinctive uniform, in a hue of grey (Brethyn Llwdy) and nothing like the rest of the British Army in the wearing of khaki. This never materialised and the Welsh units became part of the British Army.

Sourced from the diary of Sergeant Thomas Price, 13th Battalion (2nd Rhondda) Welsh Regiment.

"After the best part of two days we were able to give numbers to all the men and allocate them units. In effect, I took part in the formation of my own battalion, a fact of which I feel very proud".

"After two weeks at Sophia Gardens, we were marched from the camp to the station, led by the band and cheered all the way by bystanders on the streets of Cardiff. We were put on a troop train and were taken to Prestatyn in North Wales. The billeting arrangements at Rhyl, our destination, were not completed in time for us on arrival, so it was Prestatyn for us".

A week later we were marched to Rhyl and were allocated billets, ten to twelve to a house and more to boarding houses and hotels. All were commandeered by the billeting officers.

Other battalions were based in Colwyn Bay, Llandudno and other resorts along the North Wales coast. The 10th and 13th battalions of the Welsh Regiment were in Rhyl and our parade ground was the promenade. I can assure you we looked a right motley crew when we assembled for our parades.

Our first parade was in our civilian suits, the ones we joined up in, which were well worn by that time and our under clothes needed changing. Anyway, we managed as best we could until the army could supply our needs.

The uniforms we were issued with at first were made up of blue serge trousers and a sort of smock coat with a Glen Gary Cap. This smartened us up a bit. We had to wait a very long time for our khaki uniforms.

We stayed in Rhyl for ten months, and apart from doing drill and marches, we could not do much training as there were no rifles available to use for several months.

We thoroughly enjoyed ourselves in Rhyl, and the girls were falling over themselves to get a soldier friend.

"We had a concert in a theatre on the prom. We had a very good male voice choir which included two exceptional singers; Private Ward Phillips, a tenor and Private Orlando Phillips, a bass baritone. Phillips was a survivor of the Titanic".

His favourite song was 'Neptune, Lord of the Sea'. When he sang it brought the house down.

*Such was the camaraderie that existed in the battalion at that time that we went on strike on two separate occasions. On the first occasion, when we had been inoculated and the next day the Commanding Officer – **Lieutenant Colonel Gifford** ordered the regiment to parade in full marching order.*

The men paraded but a lot of them without their full marching order on. When the Sergeant Major called them to attention no one moved. "What is the matter, Sergeant Major?" shouted the Commanding Officer. "The men's arms are bad, Sir". "Dismiss the parade". The men returned to their billets.

The second occasion that the men went on strike was while we were at Kinmel Camp. A certain Sergeant Major had been given promotion from outside of the battalion. When called to attention on our first parade that morning, no one responded. "What is the matter Sergeant Major?" shouted the Commanding Officer, followed by a chorus from the men "We do not like the Sergeant Major, Sir". "Dismiss the parade" came the reply from the CO. Our protest had been made and we returned to our billets."

While at Kinmel Camp, the battalion was addressed by The Prime Minister, **Mr. David Lloyd George** and after ten months at Kinmel, the battalion was moved to Winchester. They would receive their final training prior to going over to France where the war would begin.

Above: The Welsh Battalion parading on Rhyl promenade in 1914 (3)

The following men fell whilst serving with the 13th Battalion: -

Private 32964 Herbert F. Atkinson died January 19th 1916, and is buried at Merville Communal Cemetery, France.

Lance Corporal 21494 Henry W. Atkinson died of wounds 10th July 1916, and is buried Dantzif British Cemetery, Mametz, France.

Private 16090 Herbert Edward Davies died of his wounds 21st May 1916, aged eighteen and is buried at Merville Communal Cemetery, France.

Lance Corporal 33191 Henry Jones killed in action 17th September 1916, and is buried at Essex Farm Cemetery, Leper, Belgium. All these men were trained at Kinmel Camp.

Note: The camp was in the process of beginning built, hence a lot of the Welsh Regiments and Battalions were housed in billets in the local area, Abergele, Old Colwyn, Colwyn Bay and Rhyl amongst others.

Above: How well-kept the billets were, a sense of pride was the order of the day, F Company Line of No 20 Camp (4)

New Recruits Arriving at KPC

Recruits are arriving in batches from all over the globe, **Lt Roberts** of No2 Camp is very kind to the men arriving from Corwen. He sees that they are conveyed up to the camp and not marched up, unlike some of the poor beggars.

CHAPTER 2

RHYL 1915

Extracts from the Flint Observer (May 1915)

The town of Rhyl saw great unrest during 1915. There was a riot which was sparked off by a comment made by man on the bridge in the town. The riot was between civilians and soldiers from nearby Kinmel Park Camp. Severe aggression was made toward one individual from the town. The gentleman was of German extraction, a Mr. Fassy. The soldiers later attacked the business of Mr. Robert Fassy which was situated at 35, Queens Street. Breaking the windows of his shop, the soldiers also carried away various items from the shop window displays, the cost of the items taken, amounted to £45. The family were removed to Rhyl Police Station for their own safety. The soldiers attacked the Police Station breaking windows and other items belonging to acting Sgt Foulkes (Flintshire Police). The estimated damage was about £6. Several attempts were made to break into the station by the soldiers through the now broken windows, but this was thwarted by the officers inside. Some of the Police Officers were roughly handled and some assaulted. An armed guard was sent to assist the police, but this proved to be quite useless in bringing calm. Later in the evening, Brigadier General R. H Dunn arrived at the scene and spoke with the soldiers and ordered them to fall in on Bodfor Street, which they did. They were then marched along the promenade and then back to their billets. Mr. Fassy his wife and two children were then taken to Victoria Avenue that same night to stay with relatives. The family left Rhyl for Birmingham the next day.

Foolish Piano-Tuner

Scenes were witnessed in Rhyl as a piano-tuner (a Londoner) had been spouting his mouth off at the objection to his military service, on Rhyl Bridge he was overheard to say "that if he was compelled to become a soldier he would fight for the Germans", also stating that "Kinmel Park Camp would be blown up". This event was reported to a military patrol by an Ada Rayner of the Toll

House, who happened to be on the bridge. They arrested Mr. Arthur Robert Brougham of Pier Cottage, Foryd. He was escorted to the local Police Station by **19819 Sergeant James Fielding** (15th Service Battalion, Welsh Regiment) along with **19115 Private Thomas Howard Evans.** The incident was reported to **Brigadier General R. H Dunn** commanding 129th Infantry Brigade. He was informed by telephone; the General ordered that Brougham be detained and examined by a doctor. Mr. Brougham was detained until the 22nd May, and was served with an order by the Military Authority (**General Phillips**) which informed Brougham, that he was not to reside in the counties of Carnarvonshire, Denbighshire and Flintshire. He was then released from custody and escorted to Rhyl Railway Station, were he left on the 1730 train to London.

'The Coldest Place in Wales' Bill Baxter's Story

Private William Baxter of the Royal Welsh Fusiliers made a statement that Kinmel was the coldest place he had ever been in. Throughout the December of 1916 he had worked every day, without a break, during heavy snowfall. He remarked that the camp, being new and incomplete, offered few comforts. He had returned from a week's leave in London, where a Zeppelin appeared overhead. He commented "that the open air in North Wales had made a wonderful difference to his health". He reflected on the Welsh having their own language, which made it hard to understand them. He went onto to state that he had "no stripes up" (promotion) and how he didn't intend to get any if he could help it. A large majority of soldiers did not want the responsibility of promotion as there was no monetary value to holding a promotion.

Julian Putkowski

'The Kinmel Park Camp Riots 1919, written by **Mr. Julian Putkowski**, is available to purchase on many well-known online book stores. It has a comprehensive summary of events therein of the riots. It is well worth a read for any military historian. Also **'The Story of Kinmel Park Military Training Camp 1914 to 1918'**, by **Mr. Robert Griffiths.**

The Canadians

The rioting of Canadian troops was caused by the cancellations of the ships 'Northland' and 'Haverford', which should have sailed from Liverpool with more than two thousand two hundred troops on board, and back to Canada during February 1919. Also involved in this episode were the 'Mauretania', 'Aquitania' and 'RMS/SS Olympic'. It should be noted that the RMS/SS Olympic did one last crossing with Canadian troops on board by kind permission of the British Government after the rioting. This was done in order to clear the back log of men. The RMS/SS Olympic had been scheduled to carry American troops home. Few of these troops could match the war service experienced by the Canadian Expeditionary Forces. In the eyes of most Canadian soldiers, this was unacceptable turn of events, given their services.

Also contributing to the upset was the fact that some soldiers had not been paid on time, in addition to feeling as though they had been 'fleeced', by over-pricing by the shop owners in 'Tin Town' (a small town built up by local merchants, built mainly outside of the confines of the camp) and the YMCA. Adding to this. was that the shipping program for repatriation being regarded by many as totally dysfunctional.

The combination of dissatisfactions resulted in the Canadian soldiers displaying their frustrations through rioting in order to get their point across to the Military authorities.

Above: The RMS/SS Olympic (5)

Chester Greenwood's Story

Here follows some reminisces of the riot, documented in October 1978, **Mr. Chester A. Greenwood** of Brantford, Ontario, Canada had been visiting the Graveyard at Bodelwyddan. The interview he gave is captured in an article entitled 'Canadian Corporal Remembers the Kinmel Rebellion' he states:

"I was in the Guard Room when the trouble started. The duty Sergeant disappeared into the melee, the rioters ran between rows of huts smashing everything in sight.

The camp master switch situated in the Guard Room, had been switched off by an electrician, plunging the camp into darkness. It was at this point that the rioters marched to the Guard Room and demanded the lights be switched back on.

At times the noise was frightening; at first light the camp was a shambolic state with rocks strewn all about. Also, some Mils Bombs (Hand Grenades) were found lying about, these where later buried in a wood close by.

A handpicked detachment of men was armed and proceeded to Camp 4 as there were rioters mustering, in the area of the training trenches. This is where the riot ended, with the whole area being sealed off. We were told that anyone trying to enter the cordoned area were to be shot on sight. Official reports state that three men had been shot and two bayoneted all died of their wounds".

One grave stone has the following inscription upon it 'Sometime we will understand. Killed at Kinmel Camp, defending the honour of his Country'.

Another article from the Rhyl Journal, dated 3rd October 1990:

'An Old Soldier Fights to Clear his Name'

*A First World War Canadian veteran convicted of taking part in the Kinmel Park Riots, **Mr. Ron Henley** of Sidney, British Columbia,Canada. Ron joined the Canadian Expeditionary Force at just sixteen and was wounded twice, he was a survivor of 'Vimy Ridge'. **Mr. Henley** went onto to serve in WW2 gaining the rank of Warrant Officer Class One.*

Ron was just eighteen when charged with rioting at Kinmel Park. The outcome of his plea is not known.

The following is a report written by **Major C.W Hodgson** the Officer Commanding No 7 Military District, it was written on the 6th March 1919, and written to The Headquarters, Canadian Troops at Kinmel Park Camp.

In compliance with your request over the telephone this morning. The following is my report on the disturbance of *yesterday. On the night of the 4th and 5th everything was quite in the camp. On the morning of the 5th March I attended a meeting of Wing Commanders, at 9 o'clock (0900 hours), at Headquarters with reference to the rioting of the night before. On returning from the meeting I called a meeting of my officers; just as the officers had assembled in the Mess, words reached me that a large mob of rioters had left camp 18 and were about to attack our canteen, we at once dashed over there.*

Lieutenant McFadyen *was standing with his back to the door keeping them from breaking in. We called on the men of Military District*

No 7 to help us which they did, some of the rioters got into the canteen but were knocked down and put out.

Very little damage was done except from bricks thrown at the windows, we talked to the rioters who all finally dispersed, in threes and fours. We had not had time to tap the beer which was still intact.

I then phoned Headquarters and reported what had happened and got permission to issue my men with beer for dinner. There was only just enough in the canteen to go round. I went round to each mess hut at lunch and talked to the men.

I told them what damage had been done in the area and asked for their support in case the rioters returned. All the men in three of the huts cheered and clapped. In the fourth hut there were two or three agitators, who made complaints about their food, but the general feeling of the huts was against the rioters and against the men making the complaints.

I told the men on the one o'clock (1300 hours) parade I would call for volunteers for piquet's to protect the camp.

At one twenty (1320 hours) the rioters came through the camp and smashed in the windows of the Warrant Officers and Sergeants Mess and knocked out the frame work and badly wrecked the Mess, another party went to the Guard Room. The Sergeant of the Guard refused them admission, and told them that there were no prisoners there, allowing one man to go in and see for himself. While the others waited outside, they broke all the windows in the Guard Room and then moved onto the next camp.

Soon after shots were heard and a few bullets passed through our camp, two men were killed and a number were wounded. **Private Walsh** was wounded and taken prisoner in the lines of Camp 20.

A total of **twenty-three** men were injured, plus **seventy-eight** were arrested (including civilians) **twenty-five** of them were courts martialled and sentenced from between eighty days in prison to ten years penal servitude. Between eight hundred and a thousand men took park in the riot, with thousands more as stand byers. (Note: none of *the civilians were charged with the event). It is regrettable that the officers charged with the responsibility of managing Kinmel Park Camp did not ensure that the soldiers and their concerns were understood, if not addressed or acknowledged. It should be noted that it was originally envisioned that the soldiers of the Canadian Expeditionary Force should sail directly back to Canada from France.*

However, a great many Canadians had relatives in the United Kingdom whom they wished to visit before returning to Canada.

General Sir Arthur Currie GCMD, KCB requested to the then Secretary of State for War (**The Earl of Derby**) that the Canadian troops should transit through the United Kingdom before repatriation. Hence a large concentration area was created at Kinmel Park Camp for this purpose.

The statement of **Private A. L Wallace** of the 15th Battalion CEF is as follows:

I was registered into this camp on the 21ˢᵗFebruary 1919, I am presently billeted in Military District 2, hut fifteen. I am a repatriated Prisoner of War.

"The situation as I see it was that there were mumblings of soldiers there were discomforts of various sorts and many men were broke, they could not purchase cigarettes or soap. We were all looking forward to getting away home", and all these things were suffered with the hope in view of something better to come in the shape of sailing home.

The Court of Enquiry Kinmel Park Riots was presided over by **Brigadier J.O MacBrain CB, CMG, DSO**. The statement heard by the Court of Enquiry at Kinmel Camp in March 1919, of **Sergeant Bremmer** the Provost Sergeant of Depot 6, Camp 19:

"On Wednesday 5ᵗʰ March at 1430 hours the rioters marched out of Camp 20. They started to raid the officer's mess and were immediately set upon by the boys of Camp 20. A few were arrested and placed into the guardroom of Camp 20, the remainder made good their es-

cape across the field opposite".

"The rioters re-organized themselves and marched toward Camp 20 with rifles etc. I (Bremmer) was standing talking to **Mr. Carlisle** when he told me to go along with him. I did so, and joined in the attack against the rioters, capturing one of them whom I marched to the guardroom. I then returned and found the rioters using live ammunition".

"I returned to the guardroom to get a rifle and four rounds of ammunition. But when I got back the boys had charged and rushed back into Camp 20, inflicting casualties amongst the rioters. When they were beaten they raised the white flag".

"I immediately rushed out and placed under arrest all the men I noticed to be with the rioters. I had some escorted back to Camp 19's guardroom, were all valuables were taken from them. One of my prisoners was sent to the hospital and the remaining five were handed over to the Regimental Sergeant Major".

Note: Sergeant Bremmer then stated that he had obtained ammunition and that his men were actually firing at the mutineers. This was corroborated by **Captain Douglas Forbes-Scott**.

Sergeant Roberts of Camp 19 testified:

"On Wednesday at 1530 hours I was one of a party detailed by Military District 6 to repel rioters endeavouring to invade the camp. **Private David Gillan** and myself (**Sergeant Roberts**) along with serval others advanced across the training ground towards the Army Service Corps stables were the rioters where hiding".

"Many of them were advancing carrying red flags, in open order, with leaders, and were armed, firing live ammunition. Twice they were driven back by Camp 19 and 20 men. After the capture of some of their leaders a white flag was shown. Of the twenty-two rioters captured, seven were by us, and fifteen were captured by Military District of Camp 20".

"During the fight Private Gillan was stuck by a bullet in the neck. I saw one of the rioters deliberately taking aim in the kneeling position. But just then another party came from behind us and we fled, leaving Gillam".

Note: Medical evidence submitted to the inquest stated, that Gillam was shot from behind, possibly from Camp 20. Seventy five men were charged with mutiny. The enquiry was presided over by **Major General Sir H.E Burstall KCB, CMC.** The Courts Martial was also presided over by Burstall held between 16th April, and 7th June 1919.

Burstall tried thirty-eight cases, involving fifty men, all of whom were charged with mutiny and other offences. Seventeen men were acquitted, twenty seven where convicted of mutiny, and six were found guilty of minor offences. Those found guilty were given sentences from ninety days to ten years imprisonment. The Coroners Inquiry was a travesty, as many witnesses had been spirited away with the five thousand Canadian soldiers on board the RMS/SS Olympic, only the previous week to the proceedings of the Inquiry.

Note: The local police had issued a summons for **Sapper 249685 M Chaka** (of Camp 11) to attend as a key witness. However, Chaka had sailed for Canada on 13th March, rendering him unable to attend.

The Bogus Staff Captain's Inspection

Mr. Henry Alexander Chamberlain posed as **Staff Captain Stewart,** and gained access to Kinmel Park Camp. He had ordered a Private soldier who was based in Wrexham to be his driver. Once in the camp, he caused much discomfort amongst the junior officers. He found fault with just about everything and everybody on his bogus camp inspection. While returning to Wrexham, the vehicle he was in, collided with a tramway car. The vehicle Chamberlain in was badly damaged. Chamberlain was quick to act, ordering some soldiers which were travelling on the tram car to guard his vehicle overnight, telling the soldiers he would square things up with their officers, which he did.

This incident aroused the local authorities, the net was closing in on Chamberlain. While in the company of regular officers in Rhyl, Staff Captain Stewart was arrested by the Military Police who then handed him over to the constabulary at Rhyl. Whilst in police custody, his past was beginning to catch up with him with various felon's coming to light.

There were three county court judgements, those of Gloucester, Suffolk and Devon to whom he had to answer to. Chamberlain eventually appeared at the Magistrates Court, Machynlleth on the 22nd July, 1915.

With above three mentioned county court charges pending against him. He was committed for trail and would remain in police custody until a date could be set.
In late October 1915, Chamberlain appeared at Ruthin Assizes in North Wales. Where he was described as an audacious fraudster. The judge passed sentence on all charges including those pending, which also included a case of bigamy, to 5 years of penal servitude.

Chapter 3

Kinmel's Visitors from Canada

The 'BIG' Four

Four wartime pals who referred to themselves as The 'BIG' Four, formed their friendship while at Deepcut, Hampshire, prior to deployment to France in 1917. The friends were all Royal Canadian Artillery men: **Private 'Cam' Cameron, Private 210083 'Mex' Bosedet, Private 'Dreamer' Fisher, and Private 'Yank or Yankee' Cate.** Private Mex Bosedet was wounded on the 16th September, 1918. His knee being smashed. He joined his buddies at Kinmel Park Camp prior to returning to Canada, were they all remained good friends.

A Very Short Stay at Kinmel Park Camp
Hopcraft J.

Corporal 404117 Hopcraft J of the 3rd Battalion the Toronto Regiment, had a very short stay at KPC, just 5 days before he was repatriated back to Canada. He arrived on the 5th December, 1918 He left for Canada on the 10th December, 1918. On board 'HMT Melitn'. Hopcraft had been wounded twice during his service in France and Belgium. On the first occasion he was hospitalized in the UK for twelve month period.

9th Canadian Field Hospital

For almost a year the Canadians had a field hospital at Kinmel Park. It was commanded by **Colonel E. G Davies** and by **Colonel E.J Williams.** The **Matron** during this period was a **V. C Nesbitt.** The Queen Mary's Auxiliary Corps had a depot at Kinmel Camp. There were also local civilian nurses employed to work at the camp.

The following are extracts from the (CMD) Canadian Military Districts Diaries:

On the 11th December, 1918 Camp twenty of the Canadian Military District, was taken over by **Major C. W McLean**, *of the 12th Reserve Battalion, from* **Captain W.C Sterling** *The Manchester Regiment at 10 am. At 1730 hours four men arrived having marched from Abergele to Kinmel Camp.*

On the 14th December **Lieutenant G. Beaudry** *1st Tanks arrived for duty.*

On the 15th December **Lieutenant W. Campion** *2nd Tanks arrived for duty.*

On the 15th December, 1918 an Ordinary Rank was tried in Civil Court charged with stealing a bicycle, found guilty and sentenced to three months hard Labour.

On the 20th December all Canadians of Polish Origin are to be given the opportunity of transferring to the Polish Army, before being returned to Canada.

31st December 1918 two Buglers are taken on strength as permanent cadre. It is good timing as they may employed appropriately.

On the 12th December (sailing number 96) 268 men from Canadian Military District 6 left camp along with 182 men from Canadian Military District 7 for return to Canada.

On the 14th December Number 7 Wing opened for the New Brunswick Troops. The Officer Commanding was **Major C. W Hodgson** *and his second in Command was* **Captain Cameron.**

On the 14th December Number 10 Wing had the following Officers appointed, Officer Commanding **Captain J Grindly** *(Canadian Field Artillery), Second in Command* **Lieutenant R.S Edwards** *(GMGD),* **Regimental Sergeant Major 431437 K Matheson** *(42nd Battalion).*

On the 21st December, 1918 **Lieutenant's, Armstrong, McBeath,**

Dixon, Gibson Hillier and Simpson and 300 Ordinary Ranks were to proceed to Canada on sailing number 99.

On the 16th December a full kit inspection called for all ranks in Canadian Military District 6.

*Between 29th and 31st December the following Officers became attached to Canadian Military District 6, **Captain White, Lieutenant G.R Smith, Lieutenant Staynor, Captain D.F Scott and Lieutenant F.H McLean.***

The above short stories were taken from the War Diaries of 9th Canadian Field Hospital.

Above: Bombardier Thomas Cains, Canadian Field Artillery CEF, was one of many Canadian soldiers to be at Kinmel Park Camp (6)

Some Canadian Soldiers who stayed at Kinmel Camp awaiting repatriation to Canada:-

David Beaton Anderson

Private 198234 David Beaton Anderson of the 5th Canadian Infantry Battalion, formerly of Rainy River Ontario, born 10th November, 1874 in Kirkcaldy, Fifeshire Scotland. He attested to the 94th 'New Ontario' on 25th November 1915. Anderson embarked from Halifax, Nova Scotia, 28th June, 1916. On the RMS/SS Olympic along with 36 officers and 1009 ordinary ranks arriving in Liverpool 6th July, 1916.

Once in the United Kingdom, the 94th were broken up. Anderson was transferred to the 5th Canadian Infantry Battalion on 5th October, 1916. Shortly afterwards, he was admitted to No13 General Hospital at Boulogne on 16th October, 1916. From there he was sent back to the United Kingdom on board hospital ship the 'St. Andrew'. He was admitted to Queen Mary's Hospital at Walley, in Lancashire. He was diagnosed with a very large 'Varicocele' to his testicles. After 24 days of treatment he was moved to The Canadian Conversant Hospital at Woodcote Park, Epsom. He stayed there for 10 weeks. Afterwards he moved onto the Canadian Causality Assembly Centre. After quite some time spent there, he moved onto the Canadian Artillery Service Corps Deport at Blandford, Dorset. He eventually ended up at Kinmel Camp on the 20th May, 1919. He embarked to Canada on board the 'SS Lapland' 2nd June, 1919.

Note: Anderson was never involved in any fighting; in fact he served only eleven days in France. He was awarded the British War Medal and the Victory Medal.

Fred Theodore Clark

Private 877747 Fred Theodore Clark of the 25th Infantry Battalion (Nova Scotia Rifles), born 14th June, 1885. In North Sydney, Nova Scotia. He was attested to the 185th Infantry Battalion (Cape Breton Highlanders) on 23rd March, 1916. He sailed with his battalion from Halifax later that year on 12th October, arriving in Liverpool five days later on 18th October. After some months training in the United Kingdom, he was transferred to the 25th Battalion arriving in France 28th April, 1917.

Amazingly Clark was declared unwell on 28th April, 1918, with venereal sores. He was sent to the United Kingdom for medical treatment, returning to the 54th on 2nd September, 1918. Just two days later, he was wounded with a gunshot to his left hand. He was sent to Woodcote Park to receive treatment and on 10th December, 1918, he was transferred to Kinmel Camp. On 12th December that year he was assigned to the 17th Reserve Battalion. Fred returned to Canada 5th January, 1919, on the RMS/SS Olympic. He took his discharge from the army 8th February, 1919.

Victor Egleston

Lcpl 213281 Victor Egleston born 4th April, 1897. In Hoo, Kent. He was attested to the 99th (Essex Battalion) 14th, 1915. In Windsor, Ontario. He sailed to the United Kingdom on the SS Olympic 31st May, 1916. Under the command of Lieutenant **Colonel T.B Welch**. 36 officers and 825 ordinary ranks sailed, arriving in Liverpool 8th June, 1916. The battalion was absorbed into the 35th Reserve Battalion on 6th August, 1916. Egleston suffered a severe gunshot wounds to his chest and face on 15th September, 1916. He was transferred to the United Kingdom CCAS at Folkstone, Kent. From there, he was sent to the 3rd Canadian Reserve at West Sandling Camp. Egleston was sent back to France and the 19th Battalion. He was later hospitalized again on 16th November, 1917. This time he was suffering with trench foot. He was at Sandling for five months before being promoted to Lance Corporal and moving to Kinmel Camp in North Wales. Whilst in hospital in the UK he was diagnosed with 'Pulmonary' He was discharged by the Medical Board 3rd February, 1919. Egleston died on 15th September, 1934, eighteen years to the day from his original hospitalization. His mother, **Mrs. Anna Egleston**, received his memorial cross, as the army accepted responsibly for him.

Harry Wallace Wilson

Private 1477 Harry Wallace Wilson was born June 12th, 1896. In Gateshead, Newcastle-on-Tyne, England. He was attested 7th December, 1916 in Toronto into the 2nd Canadian Field Bakery, aged 18 years.

Wilson was admitted to No11 General Hospital at Boulogne suffering from 'Myalgia' (muscle pain, a symptom of many diseases and disorders). He was discharged on 21st May later that year. He was admitted to No14 General Hospital at Wimereux the following winter, on 11th January with 'Scabies'. He was discharged 25th January, 1917. He was then transferred to the Canadian Army Service Corps and stuck off their strength, returning to Canada. He was then medically discharged on 8th , 1917.

Wilson re-enlisted in the Royal Canadian Dragoons shortly after on 29th May 1917, just two weeks shy of his 21st birthday. He arrived in Liverpool on 18th March 1918 with the RCD's and was posted to Somerset Barracks in Shorncliffe, Folkestone. He was then transferred to the Canadian Machine Gun Corps at Maresfield on 20th May, 1918. From there he was sent to the Machine Gun Cavalry Squadron.

On cessation of hostilities he found himself at the Canadian Machine Gun Depot, before eventually ending up at Kinmel Camp in North Wales on 15th May, 1919. Before his repatriation to Canada.

Gunner 153 Percival John Howard, Military Medal

Gunner Howard of 8/a Brigade Canadian Field Artillery. He was born 8th June, 1895 in York Township, Ontario. Howard enlisted into the 2nd Division Signals Corps on 12th May, 1915. Aged 19. He arrived in the United Kingdom, Liverpool on the 'SS Megantic' of the White Star Line on 24th May, 1915. He embarked for France on 10th January the following year and was taken on strength with the Canadian Army Vetnary Corps 1st Division. After almost three years he arrived at the Canadian Corps Artillery pool attached to the 8th Army Brigade Canadian Field Artillery as a gunner, on 17th April, 1918. Gunner Howard saw lots of action in the autumn of 1918. Subsequently, he was awarded the Military Medal for bravery in the field at Amiens. He was gazette on 18th Friday October, 1918. His last posting was to Kinmel Camp, arriving there on 11th March, 1919. He embarked for Canada three months later.

Charles Melbourne Johnson

Sergeant Charles Melbourne Johnson of the 4th Siege Battery Royal Canadian Artillery, left St. Symphorien on the 29th March, 1919. Arriving at Kinmel Camp in North Wales some time later.

Charles missed the riots, no sooner had he arrived at Kinmel he was then transferred to Southampton, readying himself for embarkation to Canada. He sailed on HMS Mauritania on the 9th May, 1919. This is just one of many examples of just how quickly service personnel were moving through the system after the Tribunal and Courts Martial at Kinmel.

Private 838301 Thomas William Holmes, Victoria Cross

Thomas born 27th October, 1898. Montreal, Quebec, Canada, to parents John and Mary E Holmes. He enlisted at Owen Sound, Ontario (380, 9th Street East, Owen Sound). Posted to France as part of the 147th Grey Battalion). He was sent to the 4th Mounted Rifles. He fought with 4CMR at 'Vimy Ridge' where he was wounded in the forearm by machine gun fire. He was subsequently sent to the UK for treatment of his wound. After convalescing he returned to the 4CMR ready for the battle of Passchendaele. (3rd Ypres) he was awarded his Victoria Cross on the

26th October, 1917. (London Gazette No 30471, 8th January, 1918).

Which reads: -

Private 838301 Thomas William Holmes

For most conspicuous bravery and resource when the right flank of our attack was held up by heavy machine gun fire and rifle fire from a pill box strong point. Heavy casualties were producing a critical situation when Private Holmes, on his own initiative and single handed, ran forward and threw to bombs, killing and wounding the crews of two machine guns.

He then returned to his comrades, secured another bomb, and again rushed forward alone, under heavy fire and threw the bomb into the entrance of the pill box, causing the nineteen occupants to surrender.

By this act of Valour at a very critical moment, Private Holmes undoubtedly cleared the way for the advance of our troops and saved the lives of many of his comrades.

Tommy was promoted to the rank of Sergeant. He to was sent to Kinmel Park Camp for processing and being repatriated back to Canada. He left the UK on board SS 'Saturnia' on the 30th March 1919, finally arriving in Owen Sound on the 14th April 1919, to a hero's welcome.

After a ten-year battle with cancer, Tommy last fight was over, passing away on the 4th January 1950, at Sunnybrook Hospital, Toronto. He was buried with full military honours.

As an afternote, Tommy's medals were stolen from his home in Owen Sound, his medals have never been recovered.

Sergeant 830651 Alexander Picton Brereton Victoria Cross

Alexander Picton Brereton was born 13th November, 1892. At Oak River, Manitoba, to Cloudesley and Annie Frazer Brereton (nee Black). He enlisted at Winnipeg into the 8th Battalion (90th Winnipeg Rifles). Arriving in England aboard RMS Olympic on the 25th September, 1916.

Alex was promoted to Corporal during the battle of Amiens (8-11th August, 1918) It was during this battle that he was awarded his Victoria Cross.

His citation reads as follows: -

For most conspicuous bravery during an attack, when a line of hostile machine guns opened fire suddenly on his platoon, which was in an exposed position, and no cover available. This gallant NCO at once appreciated the critical situation and realised that unless something was done at once, the platoon would be annihilated. On his own initiative, without a moment delay and alone sprang forward and reached one of the hostile machine gun posts, where he shot the man operating the machine gun and bayonetted the next man who attempted to operate it. Whereupon nine others surrendered to him. Corporal Brereton's action was a splendid example of recourse and bravery and not only undoubtedly saved many of his comrade's lives, but also inspired his platoon to charge and capture the five remaining posts.

Alex spent some time at Kinmel Park Camp (MD 10) awaiting reparation to Canada, sailing on HMT 'Empress' on the 17th February, 1919. Disembarking on the 25th February, 1919. He went on to serve in the Second World War, gaining the rank of Company Quarter master Sergeant. He died on the 10th January, 1976. He is buried at Elnora Cemetery, Elnora, Alberta. His medals are held with the **Lord Ashcroft** collection at the Imperial War Museum, London.

Private 3206893 Victor B Moren 21st Battalion CEF

"Did you shoot any Germans Uncle Victor"

Private Moren born 13th April, 1891. In Jonkoping, Sweden. He attested at Edmonton, Alberta 21st November, 1917. Into the 21st Battalion CEF.

The following was written by his Nephew Carl E. Moren.
The question was asked "did you shoot any Germans" with Victor replying "I hope to God I did not, but I may have, we all shot a lot towards their trenches. We stretcher-bearers got the worst of the rifles and mine was no exception, but I may have. War is ugly with mud, blood, guts and death to most, sooner or later".

After a short while Uncle Victor continued, "I will tell you of an incident I was involved in, I hope it will never happen to you", he said.

The section of trench which Victors Company was under constant machine gun fire from a German-pillbox, if any man was to pop his head above the parapet, he would draw fire. An officer realizing this, that it would mean certain death to men from his company should a direct assault be required on the enemy trench to their front.   The officer called for a volunteer, who was expected to crawl forward and throw some grenades into the position. One man came forward, he was sick and tied of war, filling a bag full of grenades and off toward the pill box he crawled, after a couple of hours the German machine gun opened-up and the volunteer was hit. His cries could be heard for the remainder of the afternoon. The German machine had by now ceased firing at him, as he was longer a threat. The Company Officer stated that a rescue party would go out that night and bring back their wounded comrade.
Pte Moren and a fellow stretcher-bearer were detailed for the recovery. This was a suicide mission for sure, as the German machine would have zeroed in on the position were the Canadian soldier fell. The bearer party began to crawl forward; this was very difficult in the darkness. They eventually reached their comrade, finding him in a terrible state. Rounds had cut

his stomach open and his intestines were spilling out. However, he was still alive and conscious. He begged the bearers to put him out of his misery, asking Victor to shoot him in the head. Victor believed the soldier would have shot himself long before, but due to the severity of his wounds he could not reach his rifle. There being no chance of moving the soldier, together with, in his opinion, it would be futile to attempt to retrieve the soldier back to their lines. To compound his decision the German pillbox realizing that a rescue mission was taking place, gave spasmodic fire onto their position.

Private Moren made the decision to dispatch his comrade and hoped to God that he had made the correct one, stating that "this action had bothered him throughout his life". An act of kindness if ever there was one. I have no doubt, that Victor was not alone in taking this action during the Great War. 'God Rest Their Souls'.

Aboriginal Veterans (First Nations) have served both in Canada's Military Forces and as allies, from the formative times of 1812 up to the present day. Their contribution was essential to Canada's survival during earlier times. It would be remiss of me not to include the names of a few Native Canadians, who served with honour and passed through the gates of Kinmel Park Camp.

Lt Charles Denton Smith MC, 20th Battalion CEF

His citation reads for the winning of his Military Cross:

For conspicuous gallantry and determination at Framieres on the 9th November, 1918. He led his platoon forward with such rapidity that he surprised a party of sappers preparing to blow up a road mine. Rushing forward, he shot the man who was in the act of igniting the fuse. The same evening, he personally captured a machine gun, disposing of the crew.

Lt Alexander G. E Smith MC, 20th Battalion CEF

His citation reads:

For conspicuous gallantry in action, he proceeded with a party of bombers and captured an enemy trench and fifty prisoners, displaying the greatest courage throughout. He was twice buried by shells , but he stuck to his post.

Some First Nations men who also camp through the gate of Kinmel park camp:

Private 739294 Enos Williams MM, 1st Canadian Infantry Battalion CEF, Private 30396 Mike Mountain Horse 50th Battalion CEF, Private 895282 Joseph Crow Chief 50th Battalion CEF, Sgt 469762 Samuel Globe DCM, Canadian Royal Engineers, Private 820872 James Redsky 52nd Battalion CEF, Private 820905 Edward Redsky 52nd Battalion CEF. There where many more first nations men who served their country with great courage and fortitude.

Some names of Canadian Officers who passed through Kinmel Camp on their way back to Canada:

Brigadier E. B Cuthbertson CMG, MVO (The former Camp Commandant), **Colonel Colquhoun Lt. Colonel J. P French, Acting Lt. Colonel H. W Harbord, DSO, Acting Lt. Colonel E. V Collier DSO, Major Weyman, Major Daniel H Sutherland OC No2 Con Coy, Major William E Kidd, MC 21st Bn CEF, Acting Major C. Stevenson, MC. Captain Samuel P. Lough, MC. Captain Arthur J. Gayfer, Captain Herbert Wilfred Kerfoot RAMC, Captain Weir, Captain William A. White, 2nd Con Bn, Captain Roberts J MC, Captain Cyril G. Lloyd MID, 1st CMR, Captain Ernest Harston CACC, Lt Gauthier, Captain William C. Sprague CADC, Lt H Perry, Lt Ernest N Halton, Lt Roderick Livingston, Lt Russell R. R Mclean, Lt James S Grant, Lt Gillian C. McLean, Lt A. M Edward, 15th Res Bn, Lt George H. Parker, Lt Alfred S. Jones 1st Canadian Pioneer Bn, Lt Denton Smith MC, 20th Bn CEF, Nursing Sister Margaret K Beard, Nursing Sister Margaret C Drew, Nursing Sister Margaret V Foster, Nursing Sister Mary G Fox CAMC, Nursing Sister Clare Glass, Nursing Sister Annie E Green, Nursing Sister Rebecca**

McIntosh, (died at Kinmel Camp), **Nursing Sister Anna C Grera De Wolf.**

The names of some Senior Non-Commissioned Officers:

Regimental Sergeant Major Brierly, Sgt Major Gilbert Smith, Sgt J.D Irving, Provost Sgt Bell, Sgt Murdock, Sgt Samuel Globe DCM, Royal Canadian Engineers, Sgt 931011 Edward Sealy No2 Con Bn, Sgt 931239 Albert M. Alberga No2 Con Bn, Sgt 707253 Alfred James Dasher, Sgt 931709 William Thomas.

The names of some Junior Non-Commissioned Officers:

Corporal 4454480 Holly J. Leet, 55th Bn CEF, Acting Corporal 2140663 J.B Morrison, Corporal 931570 Joseph R. Butler.

The names of some Privates, Sappers and Signalmen:

Private 2137797 J Golden (rioter), Private 102032 B. Bisloud (rioter), Private 64527 H.B Williams (rioter), Private Scott, Signalman 1251417 W. L Hanley, Gunner 1251433 Norman J. McLeod, 78th Bty, Private W. H Clarke 89th Bn CEF, Private P O'Reilly 56th Bn CEF, Gunner William Hinney, Gunner 326194 John F. Hickman 58th Bty, Private 820363 Robert Archie 44th Bn CEF, Private 633885 Patrick Brennan 21st Bn CEF, Dvr Percy Charlton, CFA, Private George Murray, Private 793535 Fred P Clement 42nd Bn CEF, Private Lorette, Private 210203 Costughko, 20th Bn CEF, Private 3037026 Russel H Edmondson, Sapper 2502989 Mervon English, Private Walker, Pte 847261 Wilbury Hamelin 69th Bn CEF, Private Roy E Henley 42nd Bn CEF, Sapper 279502 John Hiba, 8th Battalion CRT, Gunner 90256 George A Lorette 7th Bde Canadian Field Artillery, Private 243315 Valentina Miculka, 21st Battalion CEF, Private 187154 William R Sampson, Private 141508 Lionel J Middleton, (he married a local while at Kinmel Park Camp), **Private 190168 Douglas H McPherson 4th Canadian Mounted Rifles, Private Alec McDicken 13th Battalion CEF, Private Melvin A Steer 46th Battalion CEF, Private 75503 Edwinson 78th Battalion CEF, Private Joseph 267960 Schmidt, 29th Battalion CEF, M. Kendrick**

29th Battalion CEF, Private 199338 Charles E Oldale,

Private 4005055 George A Diestel Myer, HQ Staff, Private Patrick Martin, Private Milton Rentoul, Pte Guy Patrick, Private Herbert Rogers, Private Nicolas Landy. (The last five names were convicted felons whilst serving at Kinmel Park camp for various offences.)

The above mentioned names are but a few of the many thousands of Canadians that had passed through Kinmel Camp, by the end of The First World War.

Chapter 4

Kinmel Park Camp, 1914-18

The following British Units used Kinmel Park Camp between 1914 and 1918. First World War, units such as the 3rd 4th, 9th Battalions of the South Wales Borders plus the 53rd Young Soldier Battalion. The 9th Reserve, 10th Service 12th Reserve, 13th Reserve, 18th, 20th, 21st and 22nd Battalions of the Royal Welch Fusiliers, The 16th and 17th Officer Cadet Training Battalions, The 58th, 62nd, 63rd 64th Training Battalions. The 2nd, 12th, 13th Battalions, The Welsh Regiment, the 61st Training Unit, The 53rd Battalion The Cheshire Regiment. The Young Soldier Training Battalions, which included the 59th Young Soldiers Battalion, having no regimental affiliation, used the camp as a basic recruit training unit and so part of the 14th Reserve Brigade.

9th Reserve Battalion RWF

Formed in Pembroke Dock on the 31st October, 1914. As a service battalion of the 104th Brigade - 30 Division. On the 1st September, 1915. It became the 2nd Reserve Battalion at Kinmel Camp. On 1st July, 1915. It converted to the 57th Training Reserve Battalion of the 13th Brigade and later it became the 52nd (Graduated) Battalion.

10th Service Battalion (1st Gwent) RWF
Formed in Brecon in the October of 1914, as a Service Battalion by the Welsh National Executive Committee, it moved to Kinmel Camp in the December of 1914, under the command of 130th Brigade – 42nd Division.

13th Reserve Battalion RWF

They were formed at St. Asaph in the July of 1915, as a Reserve

Battalion they moved to Kinmel Camp on the 1st September, 1916. They then converted into the 59th Training Reserve Battalion as part of the 13th Reserve Brigade.

13th Battalion (1st North Wales) Royal Welsh Fusiliers
The 13th were raised at Rhyl on the 3rd September, 1914. By the Denbigh and Flint Territorial Forces Association, they were then transferred over to the Welsh National Executive Committee on the 10th October, 1914. In the November of 1914, they joined the 128th Brigade – 43rd Division at Llandudno who were renamed the 113th (Welsh) Division on 28th April, 1915. They were sent to France in the December of 1915.

In the July of 1916, they were in action at Memetz Wood on the Somme, suffering severe causalities. This Division did not return to major action for more than twelve months. The little village of Ruthin, not to far from Rhyl suffered terribly losing twenty six of its young men.

Twenty-two men were killed in action and four died of their wounds later.

The South Wales Borders

Above: Lance Corporal Ivor Morgan outside his billet 8th

Camp, the 12th hut, at Kinmel Camp (7)

Lance Corporal 33322 Ivor Morgan (13th Battalion) was the son of Gertrude Totterdell (married her first husband James Morgan who passed away on 8th April, 1908). Ivor was born in Tregere, Monmouthshire on 6th December, 1895. He lived in Tredegar, Monmouthshire and was employed as an auxiliary postman for four years prior to joining his regiment.

His basic training was initially at Kinmel Park Camp before being sent to one of the many camps in Brecon for further training, prior to being sent to France with his unit.

Ivor wrote to his sister Maud often and you will see some of his correspondences to her below;

Above: Addressed to his Sister Mrs. T Walters 65 High St Tredegar Mon. Posted at 2.30pm 1st August 1916, Kinmel Park Camp Rhyl (8)

The card reads as follows:

Just a PC to let you know I am in the best of health and I hope you are all the same at present. Hope to hear from you soon. Best love Ivor.

Above: Letter sent to his sister Maud from Kinmel Park Camp (9)

Private I Morgan 13th Battalion SWB. B Company. 8th Camp 12 Hut Kinmel Park Rhyl North Wales.

Dear Maud, Just a few lines to let you know that I am in the best of health, as I hope you are getting better by this time Hope all are in the Best of health. I am having a good time here now. Hope the baby is going on alright and that you will soon be about again. I wrote a letter to Mam this morning and one to Florrie on Friday. I have not much news to tell you so I will close with best love. xxxxxxx

cont. Hoping to hear from you soon you're loving Brother Ivor xxxxx for the Baby from Uncle Ivor Bow-Wow.

Above: A letter on Salvation Army Headed Paper (10)

The letter above reads:

Pte I Morgan 23322 B Company 13th Battalion SWB, 12 Hut, 8

Camp Kinmel Park Rhyl North Wales.

Dear Maud & Tom & Baby, just a few lines in answer to your most welcome letter which I received alright yesterday. Glad to hear that you are in the best of health as it leaves me at present except for that I have had inoculation again the day before yesterday and it is giving me something to go on with. Well I am glad to hear that you have found them in the best of health as I have not heard from them since I was home on leave.

I am sorry to hear that Jack has been getting into trouble again as I don't think there is too much money there now.
Well I don't think there I have any more to say this time so I will close hoping to hear from you soon. I remain your loving Brother XXXXX-XXXX Ivor XXXXXXXXXX.

Please excuse this scribbling as I have a bad arm with inoculation I had on my right arm this time. Good night and good luck to you three. XXXXXXXXX for baby George from your Uncle Ivor.

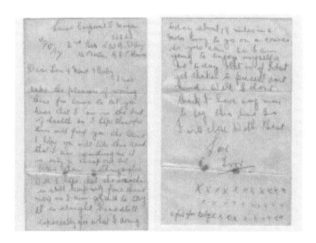

Above: Letter to his family June 1917 (11)

One of the last letters written by Ivor to his family in Wales. Lance Corporal Ivor Morgan was hit by a shell on the frontline and killed instantaneously on 4th , 1917. He is buried at Bard Cottage Cemetery in France (grave: 11-J-8).

Howell Griffiths

The Reverend W. Howell Griffiths was an army Chaplain and the curate of Ruthin. He moved to St. Asaph, N. Wales and became Chaplin to Kinmel Park Camp. He committed suicide at his father's house in South Wales on the 15th December, 1917. It was reported that he did this whilst the balance of his mind was distracted by his war work. It was not unknown for Chaplains of Military Units to take their own life during this dark chapter of our history due, to the amount of angst placed upon them by their peers and subordinates alike.

George Davies

Private 16557 Geoffrey Davies aged 18, was one of the 13th Battalion who fell on 22nd April, 1918, whilst serving in France. As did **Private 16950 Richard Evans** who died on the 1st December, 1915. Also **Lance Corporal 16834 William Evans** aged 34, lastly **Private 17402 Joseph Clifford** he died at sea on the 16th August,1915.

14th Reserve Battalion RWF

They were formed at Press Heath, in the September of 1915, as a Reserve Battalion. They moved to Conwy in the October of 1915, but then moved to Kinmel Camp in early 1916. On the 1st September, 1916. They converted into the 65th Training Reserve Battalion of the 14th Reserve Brigade.

Bringing in the Harvest

Kinmel Park Soldiers volunteer with bringing in the Harvest, taking up positions on farms on the Island of Anglesey. The following Soldiers volunteered to work on the Harvest of 1916. **Private 23140 John Jones** and **Private 43288 W Hughes** of 'A' Company 20th Battalion, Royal Welsh Fusiliers.

Signalman 40069 J Lewis, 22nd Battalion. Many young men from various camps from all over the North West were engaged in brining in the Harvest.

Parliament

On three separate occasions the Camp was mentioned in the 'House of Commons' by individual Members of Parliament. Concerns about the conditions soldiers were enduring during their time at Kinmel Park were raised.

Stanley, Henry, Parry Boughey VC

The Victoria Cross was awarded to a former Kinmel Park Camp recruit. Young Officer **Stanley H. P Boughey** was killed on active service (Boughey was at KPC from December 1916 to April, 1917). **2nd Lieutenant Boughey** aged 21 died 4th December, he is buried in the Gaza War Cemetery. He was serving with 1st/4th Battalion Royal Scots Fusiliers. 2nd Lieutenant Boughey was awarded the Victoria Cross, his citation in the London Gazette (12th February 1918)

It reads:

'For most conspicuous bravery'. When the enemy in large numbers had managed to crawl within 30 yards of our firing line, with bombs and automatic rifles, were keeping down the fire of our machine guns. He rushed forward alone with bombs, right up to the enemy, doing great execution and causing the surrender of a party of 30. As he turned to go back for more bombs he was mortally wounded at the moment the enemy were surrendering"

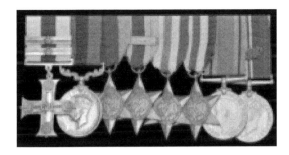

Above: Lt. Col Thomas J. Tirrell Medals (12)

Lieutenant Colonel Thomas J Tirrell, Royal Horse Artillery MC and Bar, (twice) DCM, MID. **Master Thomas Joseph Tirrell** from Yorkshire was born in 1909. He joined as a Bugler/Trumpeter when he was just seventeen. Eventually he retired from the Army as a Lieutenant Colonel. Tirrell won the Military Cross on three occasions as well as the Distinguished Conduct Medal. He was also mentioned in Dispatches. Tirrell was an inspirational leader whose quality left both his comrades and his enemies open mouthed with admiration. There is no doubt that he contributed greatly to victories such as El Alamein. He was known as one of Montgomery's greatest heroes. At the end of his military career he was posted to Kinmel Park Camp, from where he eventually retired. He resided in the area of Bodelwyddan until he died in 1995.

Albert Nevitt

I have no doubt in my mind that many former recruits who trained at Kinmel Park were awarded various medals for bravery. One such individual was Second Lieutenant Albert Nevitt, Military Cross and the Albert Medal. Nevitt won his Military Cross whilst serving with the 12th Battalion the Royal Welsh Fusiliers and appears in a gazette on the 16th May 1916, with the following citation:

'For conspicuous gallantry when leading a bombing attack upon a communication trench, all but one of his men became casualties, but

with this man he went on within 10 yards of the enemy, when he himself was wounded. He had previously showed great daring on reconnaissance missions'.

David B Milne

A couple of famous people in history found themselves going through the camp gates at Kinmel Park. **Mr. David B Milne** was a war artist from Canada (1st Central Ontario Regiment). David left the camp to return to Canada in late January, 1919. He produced 12 works of the day to day activities at the camp and its surrounding area. These works can be seen periodically at the National Art Gallery in Ottawa, Canada.

John B Priestly

John B Priestly was another famous person to pass through Kinmel Park. **J. B Priestly** became a world famous novelist and broadcaster. He was a Cadet Officer, with the 16th Officer Cadet Battalion at Kinmel Camp. Prior to joining the OCB, Priestly was a Lance Corporal.

Robert Graves

Mr. Robert Graves was a poet and novelist. He was a Captain with the Royal Welsh Fusiliers. At Kinmel, he was an instructor of young officer cadets amongst other duties and responsibilities, which include being the officer commanding No.16 Battalion.

His most famous works were 'Over the Brazier', written in 1916, and 'David' written in 1917, and 'Fairies and Fusiliers' also written in 1917. Later works include: 'Goodbye to all That', 'Lawrence and the Arabs', and 'I Claudius' and 'Claudius the God', which were turned into successful TV dramas.

Graves was friends with Colonel T.E Lawrence, Siegfried Sassoon, Wilfred Owen, Thomas Hardy and Edward Howard March (later to become Sir Edward Howard March) amongst other great poets of the First World War.

John Babcock

Lance Corporal John (Jack) Babcock (13th July 1900 – 18th February 2010), also passed through the gates of Kinmel Park Camp. He was the last known surviving veteran of the Canadian Military to have served in the First World War. Having never seen combat, Jack did not consider himself a veteran. He was born in Holleford, South Frontenac. Ontario. Canada. He served with 146th Battalion CEF and the Young Soldiers Battalion. He once made a statement about Canadian Soldiers being "a Wild Bunch". History shows this may well have been the case at Kinmel Camp. However, Jack was not one of them. He was regarded as a gentleman to the end, and in the eyes of the Canadian people, labelled a 'Hero'. John refused a state funeral, stating that all those who fought in the First World War should be recognized at his passing. John's ashes where scatted over the Pacific North West.

Above: John (Jack) Babcock. This photograph taken in 1920, after his return to Canada. (13)

John was invited to Ottawa a couple of years before his passing by the then Prime Minster Mr. Stephen Harper, as part of

Canada's Remembrance Day Ceremony 2008. Sadly, he had to stand down due to poor health. He did however take part in the proceedings by giving a live broadcast from his home town Spokane, Washington State. USA. During this broadcast he asked the youth of Canada to "**Pass the torch**" and **"Hold it high"** on behalf of all those who fell in battle.

The wording touched me deeply, and inspired me to immediately put together a memorial to the fallen. A mural was then painted on one of the walls in my Legion (Branch 178 RCL, Bowmanville, Ontario) by local artist **Mr. Todd Tremier**. I trust it will remain there for a very long time, reminding all those who pass through the branch of the great sacrifices that were made by Canadian Servicemen and women on their behalf.

Above: The author (John D Johnson) in front of the wall mural he designed and commissioned in Canada ,after hearing John's speech to the citizens of Canada. (14)

Carlyle D Chamberlain

Another individual who left his mark on me was an American citizen serving in the Canadian Army, Private Carlyle D. Chamberlain. He was born in Glengary, Ontario on the 9th March 1893. Chamberlain spent most of his free time at Kinmel, investigating archaeological sites and hill walking in and around North East Wales.

Chamberlain left his name engraved on a stone and buried it near a bronze age Cain at Ponycloddian Hill Fort, some 50 km distance from Kinmel Park Camp. The stone was later discovered in the summer of 2008 by the Clwyd – Powys Archaeological Trust. Chamberlain also served in the US Army during the Second World War. He eventually became the museum curator of Louisville, Kentucky, after serving as a police officer.

The Welsh Regiment

After a successful recruitment drive in and around Bolton in Lancashire, throughout the month of November 1914, the Farnworth Journal reported, in its November edition, that fifteen young men from the Farnworth Saints Football Team had decided to enlist into the Welsh Regiment, after listening to the Welsh Recruitment Team at Farnworth Town Hall. The following Monday, the lads met up at Moses Gate Station ready to catch the train to Rhyl in North Wales. They were to join the 12th Welsh Training Battalion at Kinmel Park Camp. Whilst at Kinmel Park Camp, one of the young chaps wrote home and requested a football. This was duly supplied courtesy of the Farnworth Journal.

Lieutenant E.W Parker Military Cross

Corporal/Acting Sergeant Parker (of the Durham Light Infantry) was taken from the front line and sent to Kinmel Park just before Christmas 1916, where he was to be trained as an infantry officer as part of the Officer Cadet Battalion.

The intake of cadets who joined with Parker were keen and serious students in the art of warfare, all trained by first class instructors.

On completion of his officer training his was sent back to the front with the 2nd Battalion Royal Fusiliers of the 29th Division. At Poelcappele on the 9th October, 1917 he was wounded for the second time, (shot through the wrist) this one took him back to Blighty.

You can read his exploits in his book '**Into Battle**' a seventeen-year-old joins Kitchener's Army.

He comments that "that we all enjoyed the varied and active life at Kinmel Camp". In his hut he had a few good men form the Royal Naval Division who had took part in the first encounters with the German Army in the defence of Antwerp.

George John Culpitt

George joined the Royal Welsh Fusiliers in 1915, mainly due to the fact that his best friend was a Welsh man, they attested on the same day. He completed his military training at Kinmel Park Camp on the 27th April, 1916. The Regimental Band accompanied the men to the station at Rhyl, playing popular Aires whilst they awaited the train to Crewe. Next was the troop train down to London, and from there onto Folkstone on the South coast. Once at Folkstone, they were issued with life belts, a precaution against German submarines who were patrolling the English Channel. Their journey took eleven and a half hours, landing in Boulogne France, eventually arriving in a tented encampment north of the town.

Ten men per tent was the order of the day but in all honesty anywhere would had done that first night as they were so tired.

The next morning, they left for Etaples were they were to draw rifles and bayonets (brand new) they were to be tented in the area of the camp known as the 38th IBD the Welsh concentration area, but this time in five-man tents. After some very serious preparation for the front they moved out on 11th May 1916. Joining the 10th Bn RWF.

Culpitt found himself in A Company along with seven men from his draft out of Kinmel Park Camp. He was sent forward and found himself in a trench close to the front line with a couple a seasoned veterans, were he gained a certain amount of moral courage as one could rely on them in a scrape.

He was wounded by a whizzbang, where he attained mainly wounds to his head and face. This wound gave him a Blighty, 'been sent back to England', initially to the Berrington War Hospital near Shrewsbury, before being sent onto yet another hospital where he was to spend the next nine weeks.

He was eventually allowed leave on 13th July 1916, his first leave in fifteen months spent in Liverpool. He left Liverpool from Lime Street Station on the 23rd alighting in, where he was to report to the military deport there. He was then retrained for service at the front. After completion of this training, he was told he was leaving immediately for the front, given ten shillings and half fare voucher for the train.

However, the cost of the fare was sixteen shillings having only ten, and a few coppers he was helped by a friend with the cost of the fare. George was not impressed, as in his opinion he was out of pocket and was serving his country at the front.

Nothing changes I guess. George was one of the lucky ones and survived the Great War.

Newspaper cutting (The Farnworth Journal):

All saints Football Club possess a splendid recruiting record, for they have now about 25 players under arms. Last year's team, which won the Farnworth Amateur Football Cup for youths under 18, had to be disbanded when the close season came, so many had answered the call, but it was hoped to get along with friendlies this season, and up to last week, six of these had been played and four won.

Then came the special appeal of Lord Derby, and 14 players decided to lay aside their football outfit, and last Saturday nine of the eleven men selected for that day's game made their way to the Farnworth Town Hall, where, with the other five, were sworn in. Thy selected the Welsh Regiment, and on Monday morning, when they proceeded by train to Rhyl, there was a stirring scene at Moses Gate Station.

There were 200/300 present including many women, relatives and friends who could manage to secure a holiday. The lads who were promised to be kept together, took with them their football, and it is expected that they will give a good account of themselves in matches against other men in khaki during their winter training. They have been billeted in huts and got into their uniforms on Wednesday. Farnworth people hope they will all do well in the game they are used to and the greater one they are preparing for and they all come out winners. The members of the club soon made themselves at home in Rhyl and have sent word that they are having a really good time. They soon found the need to use their football boots and in answer to an urgent appeal these have followed them. On Tuesday, they played the band of their Regiment, the result being a draw, and on Wednesday they were down to meet the officers.

Lewis H Cecil

Captain Lewis H Cecil was part of the successful recruitment team, recruiting the Farnworth Boys into the ranks of the battalion. He was born in Cape Town, South Africa in 1891, and was commissioned into the 15th Welsh Battalion after initial training at Kinmel Park Camp. I have followed the exploits of these young Bolton and district men, throughout their experiences during WW1 which is compelling stuff indeed.

Albert Francis

The first man to die from the Welsh was **Private Albert Francis.**

He died at Kinmel Park Camp on the 14th June, 1915. He is buried at Box Cemetery, Llanelli in Wales. Francis was a Boer War Veteran enlisting again to fight in the Great War.

David Griffiths

Private David Griffiths died just two weeks later in Bangor Hospital. He is buried at Glanadda Cemetery in Bangor, North Wales.

Herbert L Bithell

Another Farnworth man named **Private Herbert L Bithell** joined the 15th Welsh at Kinmel Park Camp. Bithell was born in Holywell, Flintshire, and had moved to Farnworth prior to the First World War. He had played football for Atherton Bolton Rovers and also for Macclesfield as a professional. Promoted, Sergeant Herbert Lewis Bithell was regarded as one of the most trusted men in the battalion. He was fatally wounded, and died at Merville Hospital, France on 18th March, 1918. It was reported that this came as a severe blow to the battalion and all who knew him.

The following young men joined the **14th Welsh:**

Private Harry Taylor, captured by the Germans at Ypres.

Private Joseph Cunningham sadly killed on the 28th February, 1916, while being withdrawn from the front line when he was a mere 17 year old.

Private 19908 Harry Dodd of Turton Street, Bolton, enlisted with his brother **Thomas**, who survived the war. Harry was killed and is buried at the Guards Cemetery, Windy Corner, in Guinchy. He was one of seven of the battalion who fell on the same day.

Private Bob Balderson joined the battalion at Kinmel Park in 1914, aged just 16. He and is buried at St. Venant Communal Cemetery. Balderson was the youngest soldier to die from the Welsh Battalions during the Great War.

Private Joseph Ramsden was killed on the 3rd May, 1915 when he was 17 years old. He is buried at Merville Community Cemetery.

Private Harry Wilkinson from Bolton was killed on the 16th February, 1916 during the relief of the 14th Welsh Battalion. He is buried at St. Vaast Military Cemetery.

Private Andrew Ward was killed on the 25th May, 1916. Ward was part of a wiring party when he was shot by a sniper. He is buried at the Royal Irish Rifles Grave Yard, Laventie.

Private Harry Williams of Ormrod St. Bolton was killed in action at Mametz Wood. A total of five Farnworth men were killed during the attack on the Wood on 11th July, 1916. Three of them were **Private William Gerrard, Herbert Walmsley** (17 years of age), and **James Walsh**. They were great pals having worked down the pit together in their home town. They were all killed by the same shell.

Private Joseph Coleman and **Private James Thornley,** another 17 year old, were also killed in action that day.

Private James Chadwick of Bolton died at the French Hospital, St. Omer on the 20th October, 1916. He is buried at Longuenesse (St. Omer) Souvenir Cemetery.

Lance Corporal John Thomas Hill, another Farnworth man was killed 3rd December, 1916, he is buried at Essex Farm

Cemetery.

At Coney Street **Private George Farrow** and his cousin **Private Herbert Farrow** were killed. They are buried next to each other at the Bard Cottage Cemetery.

Private Thomas Whittle and **Private James Coleman** were killed at Periscope House on the 17th August, 1917. Both men were from the original Bolton and District contingent.

Private Steed was killed in action and is buried at Cite Bonjean Cemetery.

The first Scotsman in the Welsh to be killed was **Private William Duthie** of Grassick, Watten Well, Aberdeenshire. He died aged 18. Duthie joined the Battalion from Kinmel Park Camp.

It is a sad, resounding fact nearly all those young men who joined The Welsh at Kinmel Park Camp at the beginning of the First World War were killed during the hostilities.
Private 20357 Joe Larkin of Bolton joined the 15th Battalion at Kinmel Park Camp in the April of 1915. Joe survived the war despite having been gassed and wounded by shrapnel to his arm. He was discharged in 1918 with a pension of 16 shillings. He died in 1957.

Former **Regimental Sergeant Major Isaac Jones** was born in Liverpool. Jones was brought up at Ystrad Farm Lanwbra, Denbigh. He joined the Army in Chester in 1884, aged 19 years. Jones initially joined the 1st Battalion (1884-1888) and later the 2nd Battalion the Welsh, where he fought with them in South Africa during the Boer War. Eventually he retired from the Army in 1909. At the outbreak of the First World War, he re-enlisted as a private with the 15th Welsh at Kinmel Park Camp, when he was 49 years old. Just two days after joining he was promoted to Quarter Master Sergeant.

Private Peter Boardman of the 14th Welsh, at Kinmel Park Camp was a prolific writer. He etched notes on the back of silk postcards, wishing his mother such things as a Happy Christmas, New Year, and Birthday 'from your affectionate son Peter'. Peter continued the tradition of sending silks throughout the war.

Private 72851 Joshua Fielding, (Military Medal) was another Lancashire lad of the 15th Battalion Welsh Regiment. Fielding joined the Army on 23rd July, 1917 and completed his training at Kinmel Camp. Joshua died in action on 8th October, 1918, aged 19 close to Villers, Outreaux, Belgium. His military medal was awarded posthumously.

Company 20959 Sergeant Major Robert Fairclough of Farnworth played an important part in the final days of the war. He joined his battalion at Kinmel Park at the age of just 16. Fairclough landed in France on the 2nd December, 1915. Within three years he had attained the rank of Warrant Officer. He was a veteran of Mametz Wood and was awarded the **Distinguished Conduct Medal** on the 11th March, 1920. Robert died in the 1950's.

In all, more than **eighty men** from the Bolton and Farnworth area were killed whilst serving with the 15th Welsh Regiment. Most, if not *all*, were trained at Kinmel Park Camp.

The numbers of Bolton and Farnworth men who served, died and gained awards for their bravery while in the service of the Welsh paint a remarkable picture. There were seven Military Medal holders and three Distinguished Conduct Medal holders.

Above: Some Bolton and Farnworth Boys at Kinmel Park Camp 1915, resting on their bedding (15)

Jack Bowen

Another sad loss I came across was that of **Private 'Jack' Bowen** of The Welsh Regiment. It was reported in the Glamogan Gazette on the 15th September, 1916. That one of the most popular young men that Kenfig Hill has given to the Army made 'The Great Sacrifice'. It informed that offical news had come to hand, that **Private Thomas John Bowen** of the Post Office, Kenfig had been killed in action; Jack, as he was known to many of his friends, was a universal favourite, his quite winning manners enduring him to all.

He was a regular attendant at St. Theoders Church and was a member of the YMCA. He joined the 20th Battalion the Welsh Regiment (Pals Battalion) on the 15th November,1915, and was stationed at Kinmel Park Camp in North Wales, before being drafted to France. He later transferred to the 15th the Battalion Welsh Regiment. Jack was killed in action in 'The Great Push' at Memetz Wood on 10th July, 1917, at the early age of 21.

Above: Private 'Jack' Bowen of the Welsh Regiment (16)

The following letter was received from his Commanding Officer to say that **Private T. J Bowen** was killed in the great fight in Memetz Wood;

> *"Please accept my deepest sympathy in the loss of a man who was a credit to his Platoon and fought a good fight.*
>
> *Needless to say, the greatest sympathy is felt in the neighbourhood with his parents and relatives in their sad loss.*

George Watkins

Private 8139 George Watkins of the 13th Battalion Welsh Regiment was a Kinmel trained soldier who was shot at dawn for disertion on 15th May, 1917. He is buried at Ferme Oliver, Elverdinge, France. There is a good possibilty he was the only soldier from Kinmel Camp to die under these cirmstances as I have yet to come across another report of such an incident in all my studies/invetsigations.

11th Battalion Welsh Regiment

The 11th (2nd Gwent) Battalion, raised in Brecon, were stationed at Kinmel Camp during the First World War before being sent to France in 1915.

Private Richard Williams formely of Glynafon, Rhydwyn, Holyhead, Anglesey was killed at the young age of 23, while fighting at Ypres, serving with B Company, C Platoon 17th Battalion the Royal Welsh Fusiliers. Richard did his initial training at Kinmel Park Camp. He joined with his friend **Lewis Jones** of Ysgoldy, Pedair, Llanrhyddlad, Anglesey. Both were killed on the 16th June, 1917, whilst serving in different Regiments. They are buried back to back in the Bard Cottage Cemetery in Belguim.

John Henry Arnold

Private John Henry Arnold born Januay 1881, was wounded probably at Memetz Wood serving with the Welsh Regiment, invalided to VAD Naunton Park in Glostershire. He served with good friends **Lcpl Keley** and **Pte Douglas**, all did their intial training at Kinmel Park Camp.

Thomas Ryan

Thomas Ryan born February 1879, did his inital training at Kinmel Park Camp February 1915 to August 1916. Badged to the Welsh Regiment. Thomas was discharged as unfit to serve, being wounded in the back by gunshot, most probably during initial training.

Thomas spent the rest of his life at Broughton House, Manchester. He was awarded a wound badge number B299615, but never served overseas.

**Above: Some very, very young men from the
Welsh Regiment (17)**

**Above: Private Richard Williams RWF is the third man,
front right (marked with a cross). This photograh
was taken at Kinmel Park Camp (18)**

German Doctor at Kinmel Park Camp

Lieutentant H Spiers of German origin serving in the Army Medical Corps, worked at Kinmel Park Camp between 17th January, 1916 and 4th April, 1916.

This upset some of his contemparies greatly, so much so it was taken before the House of Commons. One officer was said "he would resign his postion", as he felt so angry about having a German working with him. Lt. Spiers was later posted to France.

The disguntled officer said after a consultation with the Doctor Spiers, "he was found to have a temprature of 105 and was suffering from pneumonia". A further three soldiers were also diagnosed with the same illness the same day.

Private 35811 H Edwards

Private Edwards of the 14th Battalion South Wales Borderers was a holder the **Military Medal**.

Rejection Man Illegally Arrested

Sydney Goodman was arrested and taken into custody at No 7 Camp Guardroom, Kinmel Park Camp. At the time of his arrest Goodman held an 'Exemption Certificate'. He was arrested on the 7th December, 1916.

Goodman refused to obey orders and was court martialled and then sentenced to two years imprisonment with hard labour. At a later date he proved that

he did hold an exemption certificate and was released, but he was kept on the Army's B list.

Private Norman Humpreys

Private Norman Humpreys of the 13th Platoon of number two camp, Kinmel Park was taking part in a drill parade on the 9th March, 1917 when he fainted and remained unconsious for an hour. On the 20th March he was ordered to attend a sick parade and was exposed to extreme cold for two hours, before eventually receiving medical attention. At the time an exemption certificate was issued. On the 17th March, 1916 he received a notice, calling him to Hightown Barracks, Wrexham.

From there he was sent to Kinmel Park Camp, for initail training with the training Battalion SWB. Within a few weeks on the 1st April, 1916 he was admmited into the Camp Hospital, from Kinmel he was sent to Bangor, N. Wales Military Hospital. He passed away just five days later. How this man passed an army medical astounds me and considering he was the holder of an rejection certificate. Edwards died of bronco – pneumonia.

Offensive Document Posted at KPC

Questions where asked on the 27th November, 1917 by Mr. King

MP in the House of Commons in regard to a document being posted/displayed at Kinmel Park Camp.

It appeared that it was inappropraite in it's taste and contained offensive laungauge. Officer's and other ranks took time to put pen to paper to complian. Even the Commanding Officer protected strongly.

One wonders what could have upset them so for it to get as far as being disgust in the House of Parliament.

The Bogus Staff Captain's Inspection

Mr. Henry Alexander Chamberlain posed as Staff Captain Stewart and gained access to Kinmel Park Camp, he had ordered a Private soldier who was based in Wrexham to be his driver. Once in the camp he caused much discomfort amongst the junior officers. He found fault with just about everything and everybody on his bogus camp inspection. While returning to Wrexham the vehicle he was in collided with a tramway car, the vehicle Chamberlain in was badly damaged. Chamberlain was quick to act, ordering some soldiers which were travelling on the tram car to guard his vehicle overnight, telling the soldiers he would square things up with their officers, which he did. This incident aroused the local authorities, the net was closing in on Chamberlain.While in the company of regular officers in Rhyl, **Staff Captain Stewart** was arrested by the Military Police, who then handed him over to the constabulary at Rhyl. Whilst in police custody, his past was beginning to catch up with him with various felon's coming to light. There were three county court judgements, those of Gloucester, Suffolk and Devon to whom he had to answer to. Chamberlain eventually appeared at the Magistrates Court Machynlleth, on the 22nd July 1915,with above three mentioned county court charges pending against him. He was committed for trail and would remain in police custody until a date could be set. In late October 1915, Chamberlain appeared at Ruthin Assizes in North Wales.,where he was described as an audacious fraudster. The judge passed sentence on all charges including those pending, which also included a case of bigamy, to 5 years of penal servitude.

CHAPTER 5

COMMUNICATIONS

During wartime, for many servicemen and women writing poetry was a constructive and therapeutic way of passing their time. Creative writing as a way of letting loved ones know how much they were being missed. This chapter contains a collection of poems written at Kinmel Camp Park.

There is an isolated, desolated spot I'd like to mention,
Where all you hear is "Stand at Ease" "Slope Arms,
Quick March," "Attention".
It is miles away from anywhere, by God, it's a rum' un.
A chap lived there for 50 years and never saw a woman.
There are lots of little huts, all dotted here and there, I've offered
Many a prayer, for those who have to live inside the huts, there's
"Rats" as big as any "Nanny Goat", last night a sol-
dier saw one Fitting on his overcoat.
For breakfast every morning, just like Old Mother Hubbard, you
Double round the bloomin' hut and jump up at the cupboard.
Sometimes you got bacon, and sometimes "lively" cheese.
That forms Platoon upon your plate, or-
ders arms and stand at ease.

Its sludge up to the eyebrows, you get it in your ears,
but into it you've got to go without a sign of fear, and
when you have had a Bath of sludge.
You just set to and groom, and get cleaned up for Next
parade, or else it's the "Orderly Room".
Week in, week out, from morn till night, with full pack and a rifle.
Like Jack and Jill, you climb the hills, of
Course that's just a trifle, "Slope
Arms," "Fix Bayonets," then "Present"
They fairly put you through it.
And as you stagger to your hut, the

There is another kind of drill, especially
Invented for the Army, I think they call it
Swedish, and it nearly drives you barmy;
This blinking drill it does you good, it
Makes your bones so tender.
You can coil yourself up like a snake and
Crawl beneath the fender.
With tunics, boots and putties off you
Quickly get the habit, you gallop up and
Down the hills just like a blooming rabbit.
"Heads Backward Bend," "Arms Upward
Stretch," "Heels Raise," then "Ranks
Change Places," and then later on they
Make you put your kneecaps where your
Face is.
Now when this war is over and we've
Captured Kaiser Billy, to shoot him would
Be merciful and absolutely silly.
Just send him down to Kinmel Park, there
Among the Rats and clay. And I'll bet you

He won't be long before he droops and
Fades away. (ANON)

J E Bayley

Written by Private 6033 J.E Bayley Royal Welsh Fusiliers, the following two poems were penned from Kinmel Park. Both were addressed to his dear wife:

Thinking of You

When the Sun sinks in the West,
And the evening shadows fall;
I'm thinking of those dear to me,
And of you whom I love the best of all.
At eventide – O those happy hours,

When you whispered words so sweet;
And Cupid's arrow pierced our hearts,
"Entwined" till next we meet.
Whether in Camp or at drill on the hill,
My thoughts are always of you;
Counting the days until I return,
My Darling Sweetheart, True.
My heart aches for you, my darling,
For we're "getting fit" to go
With the brave boys o'er the water,
To fight the cruel foe.
If I had wings I'd fly to you,
For parting seems so hard;
So "Loving Hearts" and Kisses True,
I send you by this card.

The Soldier's Dream of Home

I dreamed a dream the other night,
and it filled my heart with joy;
the Colonel, bless his dear kind heart,
said "Take seven days leave, my boy"
just like a rolling schoolboy,
who'd been let out to play?
I danced about the dear old camp,
My thoughts were bright and gay
I'd got my "Kit" and things all ready,
My "Pass" was all "OK;"
And nothing seemed to stop me,
On this, for me, "The Day".
My dream was a home and dear ones,
My thoughts keeping time with the train
And of the jolly times we'd have,
Before "stern duty" called again.

But I woke to the sound of "Reveille"
Which quite upset my scheme;
So I send FOND LOVE by this postcard
For I found 'twas only a dream from Kinmel Park.

Writing Postcards home to loved ones was another form of communication for servicemen and women. Here follows some examples of those penned from Kinmel Park Camp, which I have come across during my research.

Posted from Rhyl 15th February 1919:

Above: Postcard sent to Mrs. Hicks 89, George St. St. Catharine's. Ontario. (18)

The reverse reads, *Dear Mother, This is where I am staying now, I expect to sail on Monday the 17th so it will not be long before I see you. Have to go up to London, Ontario to get my discharge, it will not be much trouble. Hope all is well, I am fine. Frank.*

This postcard was sent to Miss Edna Warner of London. Ontario:

Above: A 4th Division Post Card - CEF (20)

It reads, *Dear **Edna**, I am feeling fine, having a good time tonight here on camp, everyone's under the influence of liquor. Expecting to make a move anytime. From your friend **Alf Langford**.*

The following is a letter I've come by, written by Lance Corporal 4307 **J Holmes** of the 58 Training Regiment Kinmel Camp.

Mr. Smedley,

Dear Sir, Many thanks for your kind Xmas gift. I'm sure it is very good of you to think about us while, we are at war and I hope before long we shall return to Lea Mills and settle down in peace and

*comfort. Once more wishing you a Merry Xmas and New Year when it comes. Yours truly **J Holmes**. (I noted this young man's optimism with admiration)*

As a former soldier who wrote home to his family during his military service to Mum, Dad, Wife and friends of the good and bad times one was having. I feel each of the above communications in and odd sort of way.

I have found some of my old letters, post cards and even poems which I wrote home. They brought a tear to my eye I can tell you. My experiences where nowhere near as eventful as these guys.

The following postcard was sent to Miss C.C Parkstone of 3, Berwick Terrace North Hill Road, Swansea. South Wales.

Above: Post Card sent by Fred (21)

It reads:

*Hut 30 Kinmel Park Sunday: The following is what Fred wrote to his sister. I received your letter safe, sorry to hear that you have not been quiet well. I am still in good health, trusting that you (?) Are by this time. I shall be home for my last leave in five weeks' time. I shall be glad to see Gerrard in the army it will do him a lot of good. 200 young men about 30 to 35 came to our camp yesterday so Gerrard turn will not be long. I shall write again soon. Your brother **Fred.***

Above: Call of the Flag Post Card – CEF (22)

Above: Inside St. Thomas Church, Rhyl (23)

The above card was sent from a soldier in Camp 11 Kinmel Park Camp. He states to *'Dorothy that he is leaving the camp on furlough.Hoping all are well. Best of love Frank.' Post marked 15th September 1915.*

Above: Morfa Hall, The Women's Convalesent Home Rhyl (24)

A post card sent from 41741 Quickhand J to Miss A Evans of 7, Monk St Abergevenny Monthmouthshire.

The cards reads, Hut 16 Camp 15 B Coy 21st RWF. It reads as follows, *Sunday: I have kept my promise havent I, to Mum also. It is A1 here, but not at first all was so strange. Hope you are A1. I expect Aly gets quiter daily – Eh? J. Quitehand.* Note: During the Great War this building was used also a convelesant home for re-cooperating soldiers.

CHAPTER 6

CONCSCIENTIOUS OBJECTORS AT KINMEL PARK CAMP

Above: a piece of satire (25)

Kinmel Park Camp was one of Britian's primary military establishments to which men who were CO's (Conscientious Objectors), were sent after their appeal was lost at their tribunals for military service.

In late 1915, Britian was suffering very heavy war casulties and volunteers were drying up; compulsory call up became inevintable. This resulted in the NCF (No- Conscription Fellowship).

They campaigned to have a clause written into the Military Act, which allowed individuals to claim under certain conditions, exemption from military service.
The following individuals were all CO's:

Albert Ashworth NNC (Non Combatants Corps) at Kinmel Park Camp.

Mr. Albert T Ashworth aged 30, of 150 Royds Street, Rochdale, was the General Store Manager and buyer of boots and shoes, asked for a Temporay exemption on business grounds. He was granted a three month exemption, at the same time he applied to be allowed Concientous Objector status. This was granted at a later date. Albert was sent to Kinmel Park Camp on the 11th

October, 1916, as part of the NCC. He held the rank of Private, wore a militaty uniform and was subject to military discipline. His duties would have been mainly to provide labour, building, cleaning and unloading, except that of ammunition. Being part of the NCC was not easy, especially being surrounded by men destined for the front, as well as wounded soldiers returning to Kinmel Camp for convalence. At the time Albert was at Kinmel there were two other men from Rochdale. Mr. Joseph Collinge and Mr. William H Smith. Altbert remained at Kinmel until his discharge at the end of the First World War. He died in 1960 aged 73.

It should be noted that it was very rare for an NCC man to stay at one loctaion, as they would normally be moved from one establishment to another.

Eleazor Thomas

Mr. Eleazor 'Dil' Thomas (1885-1961). Thomas was a committed socialist and pacifist, a Conscientious Objector. His motives where never religious and they were driven buy a view, that war was waged on behalf of the upper classes, and to preserve the priviledges of the rich, or defending the empire, which in turn could be exploited. After refusing to obey orders at Kinmel Park Camp, he was court- martialed and sentenced to inprisonment. He spent two months at Wormwood Scrubs before being sent to the Home Office Scheme Camp on Dartmoor. After the Great War, his family were ostrasised, yet Dil went on to serve his local community as a member for Neath Town Council for over twenty years. Eventually he advanced to the position of Mayor.

Harding Rees

Above: The Rev Harding Rees (26)

The Reverrand Harding Rees (1880-1966). Rees was raised at Salem Baptiste Chapel, Llangennech. He entered Bangor College in 1916. Because of his stance as a Conscientious Objector, he was forced to three years of hard labour in Ireland. He wrote:

My last day as a student preacher in the small chapel of Pont-Bren-Araeth near LLlandeilo was in the July of 1916. Just one week later I was washing dishes at Kinmel Camp in North Wales.

I was escorted from Cardiff to Kinmel Camp with two escorts. I could not get them to help me with my belongings on the torrid road between Abergele and the camp.

I was under the rule of Rome so to speak; I was a Conscientious Objector.

During my stay at Kinmel Camp I gained both sweet and bitter experiences. It has been said that one can come across blessings in the most unexpected places and sometime times discover on the skeleton of a lion.

One of the foremost privileges of my life having been placed into the army was meeting lads from Wales, truly cultured young men and getting to know them as Conscientious Objectors.

If it were not for their company I could not have survived that fiery furnace. There I witnessed the dangerous influences of military discipline on lads some of who were barely men. There were those who did not understand our stance by showering our tents with stones.

Having spent quite some time at Kinmel Camp we were informed that we were to be taken to Ireland. We rejoiced in the knowledge that we would be leaving behind the clattering of swords.

It has been well-reported that the Conscientious Objectors were treated abominably at Kinmel Camp. Up to seventy were held in the guard rooms at any one time. CO's George Maitland, Lloyd Davies and Walter Jolly were subjected to some savage treatment by certain guards. Yet, I have found evidence to the contrary.

A statement o**f CO James Landers** refutes this, making no reference to violence or hostility. James requested absolute exemption from military service denied by a Commission. He compromised his beliefs and agreed to join the None Combatants Corps. It is believed that he agreed, so that he could provide his mother financial support. He found himself at Kinmel Camp, and, as someone who naturally followed rules, he settled in well to his new routine. Surrounded by CO's holding broadly similar views on the war, James found he had more friends than when he was a civilian. He fell in with a group the 'Plymouth Brethren', an evangelical movement who met at the Old Smithy in Bodelwyddan. He was put in charge of groups of CO's who wished to remember the Lord at the meeting held there. He was trusted to salute any officers they encountered on their way. It would appear that Lander's experience of life as a CO at Kinmel Park, may not have been as arduous as others. This could suggest that provided a CO towed the line and behaved themselves they could be treated with respect and granted certain freedoms.

Some fifty CO's presented their guards at Kinmel with an autograph album. The first page read:

> 'To Whom It May Concern, this book contains the signatures, etc. of the many CO's detained in the guard rooms of camps 5, 10 and 19'.

The album was also filled with hand written poems and ditties. Some of them were educated and well written, others were short and simple.

One statement was written in reference to Messer's **Carter and Jones** (Members of the Provost Staff) by **CO William Rees.**

> "Little thought when I was in Cardiff, beaten in a cell so dark. That such friends as Carter and Jones I should meet at Kinmel Park Camp."

This was written by **CO W. Pugh**.

> "It is at times of disappointment and suffering that character is built up and stability gained. Socialism does come by shouting."

Whether Carter and Jones sympathised with the CO's or simply felt it right to treat fellow men with compassion, we can only guess, but they must have been immensely touched by such a show of appreciation.

CO James Lander was posted to Latham Park near Ormskirk, Lancashire.

I have stated previously CO's did not stay long at any one camp, however compliant they were, with one or two exemptions I guess.

Abram Watters

CO Abram Watters, of Pilton Green near Port Eynon, arrived at Kinmel Camp near Abergele in 1917. He found the guardroom soldiers *'offering the best of friendship'.* While the military escort that accompanied him to prison *'behaved most kindly, the way that was compatible with their duty'.* This kindness was not shared by all that he encountered however, as he added that, "*it does not take much to teach a man to put his human nature into his pocket, a soldier can only be efficient when he overcomes his humanity*".

There were a total of sixteen thousand Conscientious Objectors in the United Kingdom during the course
Of the First World War. In the main, they were regarded as Shirkers or Cowards. Myself, I do not think that was the necessarily the case. Having read some of the CO's trials and tribulations, many NNC lads were sent to the front as stretcher bearers. These men were known as the bravest of the brave.

William George Durston

CO William G Durston of the 60th Training Battalion, after just 6 days at Kinmel Park Camp was Court- Matialed and sent to Caernarvon Prison for 2 years with hard labour. Durston was a staunch conscientious objector and a personal friend of Keir Hardie.

Arthur Watts

Arthur Watts born in 1888 into a Quaker family from Manchester. The Quakers strongly opposed militarism and conscription. He was called up in 1916. Arthur took an absolutist stance. He refused to take orders in the Non-Combatants Corps to which he had been initially assigned. For his stance, he was court-martialed twice and imprisoned. On the 5th September, 1916, Arthur was arrested as an army absentee and appeared at the Manchester Police Civil Court, where he was fined and handed over to the army. He was then put into the NCC based a Kinmel Park Camp, and given the number 2712.

On the 15th September,1916, (his first court-martial) he was sentenced to 112 days with hard labour at Wormwood Scrubs in London. He was then returned to Kinmel Park Camp.

On the 29th December, 1916, (his second court- martial) he revived a claim that he made at the police court trial, that he came within the exceptions to the military service act, beging a resident of Australia and only temporarily in the United Kingdom.

On the 6th January, 1917. Arthur wrote about his second court-martial. *'The court-martial on the 29th December 1916, found me guilty, but the confirming authority, Brigadier General Cuthbertson did not confirm their decision, so I have been released from the guardroom, and shall be given another formal order and have a fresh court-martial. My partial success has encouraged me to make a great effort at my next trial. I am therefore collecting all the evidence I can. I think I can establish my claim to Australian citizenship and I want to satisfy the court as to my temporary nature of my present residence in England. If I am successful in regaining my liberty (though I am not over hopeful) I shall probably re-join the FWVR work unless there seems to be possibility of being of some use in educating public opinion a little toward peace'.*

From October 1915, to January 1916, he served in France with the Friends Emergency and War Victims Relief Service. He wrote of this experience, that he was in charge of a small camp engaged in the erection of dwellings, for refugees in the Marne, whose houses had been destroyed during the early stages of the war.

On the 6th March, 1917, he was discharged from the army as his service was no longer required. After the war, Arthur did return to the Friends Emergency and War Victims Relief Service Committee, working with them from 1920-23 in famine hit Russia. He died aged 70, in 1958.

Alfred Major

Alfred Major a Conscientious Objector, on the 26th August, 1916, while at Kinmel Park Camp, he was sentenced to two years with hard labour, and sent to Wormwood Scrubs on the 4th December, 1916. He returned to Kinmel and was court-martialed for refusing to obey a military order. This time he was sent to Carnarvon Gaol on the 23rd December 1916.

Major was suffering from heart disease. He was pronounced by Army Doctors as being totally unfit for army service and also unfit for prison. I wonder if he was ever released on these grounds.

Ernest Flint

Ernest Flint of Blackburn, Lancashire a highly qualified engineer and conscientious objector. His name was brought to the attention of the House of Commons. It was said he was to be released for civil work of national importance. I wonder if he ever did.

CHAPTER 7

DOWN TIME / ENTERTAINMENT

The **18th Battalion Royal Welsh Fusiliers** are to play in Bangor this coming weekend, 2nd December, 1916. 'Bangor are the best football team in North Wales', stated in the Chronicle.

Inter Wing Soccer 1919

On 1st February, 1919, the Wing Football team was defeated by the 5th Reserve Cavalry, by a score of 3-1. On the 5th February, they lost again this time to 10 Wing. On the 8th February, a win over the ancient enemy Military District Concentration 13, to a score line of 4-1. On the 28th February, the team lost again 2-1. This was due to a misunderstanding by the referee. There is every reason to believe that the powers that be, will review the score line and grant a 1-1 draw. One wonders how this was concluded.

YMCA Cinema
The Chronicle November 25th 1916

Written in the Kinmel Camp Notes

*'It would not surprize the writer in the least that the powers that be had been sent a complaint to the YMCA in No13 Camp. **Mrs. Stone** should have realised that no building in this camp can stand such vociferous applause without falling down.*

*The concerts are improving or am I growing to appreciate them more. I was at one last week and cannot remember ever having attended one at which the audience was so appreciative and there was no room for late comers. Some silly person actually asked me which of the items I liked best. You fellows who were there will understand why I call him names that are not nice. Just imagine trying to like some items better than another of those we heard. The Pianoforte solo by **Private***

Thomas Jones *proves that we still have another pianist that can be included amongst the host of good one's the camp holds.*

Private Gornalls *recitation was delight fully funny and deserved the encore that was called for. '***The Rosary***' is a song that compelled not a few to feel rather sadder and better times.* *Lance Corporal D. O Davies* *item '***The Farmers Boy***' puzzled me a little. The readers of these notes must decide whether the Lcpl or the audience deserves the Palm. However, Davies was in fine voice and the crowd did vigorous justice to the chorus.* *Bandsman Smith's* *song was deservedly appreciated and an encore was called for. If any of the local charity concert committee's require a humorous songist, I can recommend* *Private Bendall* *his contribution to the programme provoked much merriment.* *Private Llewelyn Williams* *is a new star in the firmament and his discovery is to be congratulated and thanked, if he is to give us any more treats such as we were privileged to hear on his debut at Kinmel Camp. It appears he was discovered amongst the recruits and if he is as good a soldier as he is a singer he is in for an early promotion.*

*His first song was '***The Sunshine of Your Smile***'. The applause that followed fairly shook the roof and we asked for more, just like in '***Oliver Twist'*** we got it too. This time it was '***Irish Eyes***'. Trust a Welshman for knowing when they hear good music. The fellow was nothing less than fantastic.*

On the 24th February, 1919, an inclusion into Wing Orders read, *'Cinema Performances for Officers will be held at the Y.M.C.A every Monday and Thursday evening at 2115 hours.'*

Statement of the Camp's work load

'The unusual routine work has been performed every day, work consisted of preparing men for their trip back to Canada, guards, fatigues, piquet's and conducting parties to meet troop arrivals from the local station at Rhyl.'

This statement was written on the 28th February, 1919, as part of Unit orders.

Swimming Gala

A military swimming gala was held at the Rhyl swimming baths in the June of 1917. Soldiers from Kinmel Camp. Three hundred and eighty two of them took part in the various events and a great day was had by all.

An article in the Labour Voice (7th July, 1917). '*News of a Soldier's Eisteddfod to be held at Kinmel Park Camp*'.

'An Eisteddfod is to be held at Kinmel Park Camp, arrangements are well in hand for holding a Chair Eisteddfod on a large scale at Kinmel Park in September next and prizes of up to £100 are offered.

*The Prime Minster the **Right Honourable David Lloyd George** is expected to preside at one the meetings. It is believed that this event did not take place as no record could be found.*

*It is worthy of note that quite a number of soldiers serving at Kinmel attended various Eisteddfods and won various literary categories these included **Private Alun Mabon Edwards** of the 13th Battalion RWF the joint winner of the 'Englyn' to the President'. He also won the prize for 'Pryddest' on 'The Soldiers Life' and for this was accorded Bardic Honours.*

Convalescents Arrive at Kinmel Park Camp

The long anticipated convalescents have actually arrived. Most are from the **South Lancashire Regiment**. Some have had wonderful escapes, and a few have gained distinction in the field. One soldier was said to have been shot just below his heart. (The Chronicle)

British Soldiers who served at Kinmel Park Camp at some time

during their service. These Items are taken from local Newspapers.

Charged with Concealing 2 Royal Welsh Fusilier Deserters

Mrs. Sarah E Drake of 188 Hope Street, Leigh, Lancashire, a wife of a serving soldier (Royal Engineers and in France) and **Mrs. E. Gibson** of Cawdor Street, Leigh, wife of a soldier serving with the 5th Manchester's in the Dardanelle's were charged with wilfully concealing **Private Howard Williams** and **Thomas Roberts** of the 12th Battalion the Royal Welsh Fusiliers both stationed at Kinmel Park Camp, knowing them to be deserters.

The case against the women was adjourned for review in a month's time. The two Royal Welsh Fusiliers soldiers were taken under escort back to Kinmel Park Camp in N. Wales.

Above: Private 64378 John Worsley RWF back row on the right, born in Manchester 14th November, 1898. (27)

John Worsley

The following story has been provided by John Worsley Junior, of Prestatyn, as is the photograph above. **Private John Worsley** told his son, John Jnr, how he was originally badged to the Royal Welsh Fusiliers, but finished his war service in the Welsh Regiment. He stated that the food at the front was awful, especially the soup, likening it to boiling water with large bits of fat floating with in it. He spoke about going over the top at the Somme, "As we advanced my mates were going down all around me. All I could think that it was my turn next." John was wounded twice, once in the hand and the other in the knee. When talking about the knee wound, John said he crawled back over half a mile through the mud, until he reached a dressing station.

The visit of Field Marshal Lord French, visiting Kinmel Camp in 1916. (French was the first Commander in Chief of the British Expeditionary Forces) (28)

(QMAAC) Queens Mary's Women's Army Auxiliary Corps, stationed at Kinmel Park Camp.

Statement written in the Rhyl Journal- Women's Army Auxiliary Corps - *'Two young women from Kinmel Park Camp have been touring the Corwen District of N. Wales during the past week, canvassing for new recruits, but they report to regret to state "without any material result".*

On 11th September 1918, a recruiting rally was held at the Pwllheli Cinema. This was to help recruit more women into the QMAAC. Margaret, the wife of the Prime Minister, Lloyd George, spoke in support of more Welsh women joining, to carry out essential war work. Brigadier General Cuthbertson (CMG) Companion of the Order of St. Michael, (MVO) Royal Victorian Order of Kinmel Camp, spoke briefly about the magnificent work being carried out by the WAAC under his command.

Edward Deforges Wood

Private TR/4/13403 Edward Deforges Wood, aged 18, was conscripted into the army in late 1916 early 1917, a recruit at the 60th Training Reserve Battalion, Kinmel Camp. North Wales. Almost immediately after he died of pneumonia at the Abergele Military Hospital on 28th March, 1917. Death by pneumonia was a frequent occurrence for soldiers at Kinmel Park Camp at this time, as you will find further on. Wood is buried in an unmarked grave in the non-conformist section of Manchester Southern Cemetery. His name is on the screen wall memorial. I wonder if it still unmarked?

Albert Edward Farrow

Private Albert Edward Farrow was born in Newport, Monmouthshire in 1885 to parents **William** and **Louisa Farrow.** He had five brothers and three sisters. Thirty years on, in February 1915, he enlisted into the army. Initially with the 19th Service Battalion Welsh Regiment. He was posted to Kinmel Camp in North Wales, with the 21st Reserve Battalion.

Whilst serving with his Regiment in France, Albert became quite unwell, hence the reason he was at Kinmel. Albert was taken seriously ill whilst on leave in Cardiff, South Wales, and was admitted into the hospital in that city. There he died on 9th January, 1916.

Albert Spencer

Private 43899 Albert Spencer, **Military Medal.** Albert of 131 Mold Road, Buckley, Flintshire was conscripted into the army in 1916. He attested on January 22nd, and was called forward on 16th June 1916, as part of the 20th Reserve Battalion, Royal Welsh Fusiliers based at Kinmel Camp. He was twenty years old. After training, he was posted to the 3rd Battalion Royal Welsh Fusiliers in Liverpool for further training. He went to France on 7th June, 1917, serving with No 5 Infantry Brigade at Rouen. Whilst there, he was sent to the 9th Battalion Royal Welsh Fusiliers on 27th January, 1917. Private Spencer took part in the following battles: The Battle of Messines, The Battle of the Menin Road, The Battle of Polygon Wood, The Battle of Broodseinde, The Battle of Poelcappele, The First and Second Battles of Passchendaele and the Battle of St. Quentin.

He was wounded in his right arm on 28th March, 1918. Initially, he was treated at Camiers, before being sent back to the United Kingdom to the Graylingwell War Hospital in Chichester. On 21st June, 1918. He returned to France with the 17th Battalion. Sadly he was killed in action on 30th August, 1918. The day after, he was awarded the Military Medal. Albert is buried at the Red Dragon Cemetery in the area of Ovillers and la Boiselle.

Joseph Beard

Private 777934 Joseph Beard of the 4th Battalion Royal Welsh Fusiliers, had died of pneumonia and was buried at Northop Rd Cemetery, Flint in North Wales. Joe was born 9th December, 1899, at 52, Swan Street, Flint, the second of four children to Mathew R. B Beard and Mary Beck. He enlisted into the Army in the November of 1917, training at Kinmel Park Camp, near Rhyl. Sadly, he never saw service at the front; he was not entitled to any war medals. Yet, an impressive funeral took place on Friday 5th July, 1917. Joe was accorded full Military Honours with a firing and bearer party, commanded by Captain Armstrong. Armstrong was accompanied by Sergeant Instructor Phillips, both men were Flint men. Lieutenant Colonel Chaplin read the opening address for the service. Joe is buried with his half-brother Joseph Beck, who served in the Royal Welsh Fusiliers during the

First World War. Sadly, Joe was killed in a road traffic accident in Tyn y Morfa after the war.

Albert Butterworth

Private Albert Butterworth of the 63rd Training Battalion, joined the Army in February, 1917, no doubt as a conscript as he was just 18. He trained at Kinmel Camp in North Wales. However, in less than one month he caught pneumonia and was admitted to Rhyl Hospital. His wife Fanny, travelled to Rhyl and was with Albert when he passed away. His body was taken to Stockport on the 24th February, 1917. Albert was buried with full Military Honours.

Aaron Hughes

Private 37704 Aaron Hughes - Royal Welsh Fusiliers of Mountain Ash, Aberdare in South Wales, volunteered to join the army on 11th December, 1915, aged 22. He was called up to Hightown Barracks in Wrexham, on 28th June, 1916. He was then sent to the 12th Reserve Battalion Royal Welsh Fusiliers at Kinmel Camp for initial training.

Above: 12th Battalion the Welsh Regiment under canvas at Kinmel Park Camp in early 1915 (29)

When Hughes had completed his training he was sent to serve with the Indian Expeditionary Force on 16th June, 1916. He was

97

sent to No2 Base Depot at Makina Masus. The depot could accommodate fifteen thousand men under hut and tented conditions.

The camps were known to the soldiers who served there as 'Much in the Marches' as it could be quite swampy during the wet season. Hughes was sent up the Tigris River in November of 1916, where he joined the 8th Battalion Royal Welsh Fusiliers. The 8th were at Amara as part of the 40th Infantry Brigade. During operations to clear the area of Khudhaira Bend on the Tigris the 8th were involved. More, so to isolate the Ottoman trenches at Hai Salient (25th June – 5th February 1919). They were successful in the capture of the trench system. Hughes was admitted into hospital on several occasions with feet abrasions, debility etc.

On the last occasion, he was admitted and diagnosed with malaria. He was transferred by ship to Bombay, India. He sailed on the Hospital Ship 'Erinpuna' arriving in Bombay 25th June,1917. He stayed briefly in the Freeman Hospital in Bombay. He was sent to the Hislop War Hospital in Bolarum seven miles from Secundabad. Private Hughes died of his condition on 8th August, 1917 aged 24. He is buried at Bolarum Cavalry Barracks Cemetery (AKA as Mount Olives Society Christian Cemetery).

Frank P Lloyd

Private 76928 Frank Percival Lloyd was born in Liverpool in 1899, to Frank and Matilda Frances Lloyd. Frank Senior was an Australian. Frank junior was the youngest of three children to this family. He volunteered to join the army aged 17 and eleven months on 24th August, 1917. Initially, Frank was sent to Kinmel Camp in North Wales, as a member of the 64th Training Battalion. On completion of his training he was posted to 3rd Battalion Welsh Regiment. He was killed in action in France whilst serving with the 14th Battalion Welsh Regiment on 27th September, 1918.

Frank H Gaskell

Lieutenant Colonel Frank H Gaskell was born in 1878 to Emily and Joseph Gaskell CBE of Cardiff. In 1900 he joined the 3rd Volunteer Battalion Welsh Regiment as a Lieutenant. On the outbreak of war, he was promoted to Captain with 2nd Battalion Welsh Regiment. He was wounded in France whilst serving with the 2nd Battalion. He was sent back to the United Kingdom to convalesce. Whilst in the UK, he was promoted to Major and asked to raise the 16th Battalion Welsh Regiment (The Cardiff Pals Battalion). Oddly enough, this regiment were formed in Porthcawl. Frank was promoted to Lieutenant Colonel and appointed to the Commanding Officer of the 16th.

The Battalion moved from Porthcawl to Kinmel Camp in North Wales where they spent eight months, even,tually moving to Winchester in the August of 1915. The Regiment went to France in the December of 1915. On 15th May, 1915, Frank Gaskell was shot by a sniper while patrolling in the Moated Grange/Riez Bailluel Sector. The snipers bullet hit his ammunition pouch and it exploded. He died of his wounds at Merville Hospital on 17th May, 1916, and is buried at the Merville Cemetery. His passing was recoded as a great loss to the regiment in the Regimental Diary.

Robert Evans

Acting Lance Corporal 39082 Robert Evans 10th Battalion Royal Welsh Fusiliers formerly of Ruthin, North Wales.

He was born in Rhyl. Evans was killed in Action at Memetz Wood in France on 8th July, 1916. His body was never found. Evans served with the 10th Battalion Royal Welsh Fusiliers.

Known to his friends as 'Jack', the following poem was written by his good friend in memorandum.

At Memetz Wood

*I lost my Pal, you surly must have heard of the glorious
attack that took place by the gallant 23rd.
Midst choking fumes of Luddite and the roar of a thousand guns.
How from that line we stove all night to drive away the Huns.
That Pal of mine was killed outright by a shell as we
left the trench, he is now sleeping the long sleep in
the blood sodden soil of the French.
And when my prayers I say at night, to him my thoughts go back and
pray that God may rest in peace, the soul of my good friend Jack.*

Lance Corporal Evans can be found mentioned on the **Thiepval Memorial** to the missing.

Here is extract from the diary of Private George John Culpitt of the Royal Welsh Fusiliers.

'George joined the Royal Welsh Fusiliers with a good friend, which was typical in those days. Chapter one of his war memoir provides a rich insight into soldier experiences on route to the front line. It reads;

At length we returned from our merge leave and were officially warned for the front, we began the various preparations, such as drawing kit, etc. which every draft had to undergo.

Swiftly the days passed and at last came the 27th April, 1916 that day being the day we were to leave Kinmel Camp for France.

We were treated to a good feed in the canteen which commenced at 3.30 pm we were given by the proprietors a bag containing one shillings worth of assorted stuff. Our Platoon Captain also gave us fifty cigarettes each. We also received various boxes of fags. We were given rations for two days, bread, cheese, cake etc. The puzzle for us was where to put it all.

Having made our farewells we fell in and marched out of the canteen, we were joined by the band and the rest of the battalion they accompanied us to the station. On arrival at Abergele the town turned out to give us a great cheer, as was the custom as we entered the station.

During the short wait for the train that ensured the band played popular Aires, the train soon pulled into the platform and we all boarded, then made ourselves comfortable. We only went as far as Crewe, from Crewe we were to catch a troop train, that would take us right through to the south coast.

While at Crewe we went to the church army which was just by the station and indulged in some light refreshments which our officer paid.'

Note: this officer stayed with George and his peers until they reached Etaples Camp in France. The officer then returned to Kinmel.

Some other Units that were stationed at Kinmel during The First World War

The Cheshire Regiment

During the April of 1918, the 4th (Reserve) Battalion of the 22nd Cheshire Regiment where based at Kinmel Camp staying a short while before moving onto Tankerton in Whitstable. They were sent from Oswestry to Kinmel as the camp they were in at that time, was given up for German prisoners of war.

3rd Battalion the Berkshire Regiment

During the First World War, the 3rd Battalion Berkshire Regiment were based for a short while at Kinmel Camp.

This included **Private 6239 William C Goddard.**

23rd Manchester Regiment

E Company of the Manchester Regiment where in Camp 20, possibly for short term training.

Private/2LT, 6368 Samuel Percy Dawson MM, CBE

Extracts from the Manchester Regimental Museum & Archive

Samuel Percy was born on the 20th February, 1887, in Bury, Lancashire, to Samuel and Emily. He was one of five siblings.

Prior to the commencement of the Great War, he was employed as a bleacher, dyer and calico printer as well as an agent for a brewing company.

Later he became a travelling salesman for the brewing Company. The Great War broke out in the August of 1914, and like thousands of young men from the Manchester area, Percy enlisted into the army. He joined the 1st City Battalion on the 29th August, 1914.

Percy trained with the 16th Battalion at Heaton Park in Manchester, quickly followed by a move to Belton Park ,and then onto Grantham. He sailed for France on 8th November, 1915. As a member of IV Platoon A Company, he became a member of the Battalion signal section . He was known as 'Signaller Daw' to his comrades. On the 1st July, he took part in the Battalions attack on Montauban, where he displayed great bravery in keeping the 16th in contact with the higher formation Headquarters. For his actions on that day, he was awarded the Military Medal. (Gazetted 16th November, 1916).

He continued to serve in the 16th until 25th February, 1917. When he was selected to train as an officer. He returned to the UK to begin his training at Kinmel Park Camp joining the 17th Officer Cadet Battalion. Percy gained his commission on 28th August, and returned to France in the September 1917.

Assigned to the 1/8th Battalion, Manchester Regiment, he took part in the Passchendaele offensive. Later in the war, he took part in the retreat from Arras to Amiens and finally taking part in the Hundred Day Offensive that drove the Germans back enough, which brought about the end of the war.

After the war, he became a Captain with 8th Battalion now a Territorial Unit. In 1928, he became the Second in Command of the 8th. In 1956, he stood down as Honorary Colonel of the 8th Battalion. He was appointed a CBE in January 1968, for his services. Percy died in the April of 1975, aged 88.

A ship was named after him the MV Percy Dawson, this ship was sold to a Greek Company and renamed the Olympic.

David Humphreys

Private David Humphreys was born in Hirnant in 1886, to Robert Humphreys and Margaret Lloyd, he had ten siblings. Prior to the Great War, he was a farmer and was employed by Henry Roberts. He lived in Brynreiniog, Penybontfawr. He married Elizabeth (Evans) on the 12th October, 1914, at St. Melandell. He enlisted into the Cheshire Regiment on the 19th July, 1916. However, he was transferred into the 58th Training Reserve Battalion of the Welsh Regiment based at Kinmel Park Camp to undergo his basic training. On completion of his training, he was sent to the 2nd battalion of the Northumberland Fusiliers.

He landed in France in the June of 1918, and saw action at the Hindenburg Line and at the final advance into Picardy.

David survived the Great War. He was one of the lucky ones.

Lieutenant William Reese

William Reese was born in Newport S. Wales on the 16th September, 1884, and was the youngest son of Able and Eliza Reese of Cardiff. Prior to the Great War, he worked at the City of London and Midland Bank in Carmarthen. He was married Alice Mable (Lallie) They lived in a flat above the bank. William was one of the original officers of the 15th Battalion the Welsh Regiment AKA the Carmarthen Pals. He was trained at Kinmel Park Camp before landing in France in 1915, as part of 114 Brigade (Welsh Division). He took part in Mametz Wood where he sustained a serious concussion; he was evacuated back to Britain, eventually taking up a post at back at Kinmel Park Camp.

Sadly, William passed away from heart failure after just three days in his new post. He died on the 2nd February, 1917.

Richard Llewellyn MM and Edward Owen

Private 67621 Richard Llewellyn MM and **Private 67623 Edward Owen** (aka Bobby) were attested together in early April 1917, and badged to the 15th Battalion the Cheshire Regiment, as seen by the closeness of their army numbers. At the time of his enlistment, Richard Llewellyn was underage as he was born in the January of 1899.

In all probability, Richard was put into a young boy Battalion until he should have reached 18 years of age. He was the son of John and Mary Owen of Crown Bach, Bridge Street, Abergele. By the time Richard had joined up, his father had passed away.

His elder brother had joined the Welsh Regiment. Both lads were trained at Kinmel Park Camp, and Richard was confirmed at St. Asaph Cathedral. Many young soldiers were confirmed during their training at KPC. Once his training was complete, Richard found himself in Ireland with the Cheshire Regiment where he stayed until he reached 18 years of age. He was then sent to front with the Welsh Regiment, where his elder brother and best friend Edward Owen were serving. On the 20th October, 1918. Richard and Edward were sent forward to find a way around a German pillbox, which was holding up the advance of their unit. Sometime during this manoeuvre, Richard stepped forward where upon his best friend Edward stepped across his front only to be shot and killed. Richard was so angry by this event that he attacked the pillbox single handed, kicking the door down taking the Germans therein prisoner, for which he was later awarded the Military Cross for his actions that day.

Officer Cadet Training

The following officer cadets completed their training at Kinmel Park Camp and have been promoted to Second Lieutenants **R.K Holmes** 6th Battalion Royal Welsh Fusiliers, **R.H Humphreys** the 8th Welsh Regiment, **D Garfield** the Welsh Regiment, **C Glynne** the Royal Welsh Fusiliers, **Harry Pritchard** 12th Battalion Royal Welsh Fusiliers and **Lloyd Roberts** to 21st the Welsh Regiment.

Chapter 8

VARIOUS OCCURANCES AT KINMEL PARK CAMP

William Morgan Gould

During the third week of July 1916, **Corporal William Morgan Gould**, one of the Camps postmen was found guilty of stealing parcels and letters addressed to individuals at the camp. He was sentenced to three months incarceration with hard labour for each offence.

Richard Hyslop

Private Richard Hyslop of the South Wales Borderers, was arrested by Constable Millington from Rhyl, after hiding in the shed of Mr. J. Williams, a photographer of 23, High Street, Rhyl. Hyslop was hiding there to avoid being sent to France with his Battalion (7th Battalion SWB). Magistrates handed him over to the military in order for him to do his duty as a soldier.

Captain Blowen

Captain Blowen of Kinmel Park Camp, stated in a newspaper about the court hearing *"This man has a bad record and was convicted at St. Asaph for stealing a ladies purse, for which he was sentenced to one month in prison"*.

At the same time Captain Blowen asked the court not to imprison Hyslop, as he wanted, to escape serving. He requested they hand Hyslop over to the military authorities, and he will be off to the front with the very next draft. This was acceded to by the court.

After a very short tour of duty in the line, in France, the 7th Battalion were sent to Salonika as part of the 22nd Division. Hyslop survived the Great War.

Thomas Williams

Private Thomas Williams of number 5 Camp, Kinmel Park Camp pleaded guilty to stealing a bicycle worth £2.10s, the property of a Mr. Rose of Rhuddlan. Mr. Rose left his bike outside of the sewage works at Kinmel, returning a short time later only to find it had gone. It was later found in Liverpool, Williams's home town. Williams was found guilty of theft and sentenced to three months with hard labour. It was hoped that when he completed his sentence that he would be sent to the front. The story was recorded in the Rhyl Journal in July 1917.

Woman Deserter (Liverpool Echo 17th January 1918).

Fanny Burgess

Fanny Burgess, the daughter of an Audenshaw labourer, was charged with the Defence of the Realm Act at Ashton. She was a member of the Women's Army Auxiliary Corps, based at Kinmel Park Camp. Burgess appeared in court in her uniform and stated:-

"If I had not come home, I should have done away with myself, as it was miserable there. There was no fire or comfort and we were not allowed to light a fire until half-past-five in the evening. The boys at Kinmel were different from those at Oswestry, we were never insulted at Kinmel".

Burgess went to on make grave allegations against the male members of the staff at Oswestry, to which the camp authorities had threatened to send her back. Fanny did not much like Kinmel Camp, but she most certainly abhorred the Military Establishment at Park Hall in Oswestry, and certain members of its staff. What happened to Fanny is a mystery.

Gum Boots and Chin Straps

Sourced from a local newspaper:

Gum Boots and Chin Straps are the order of the day. The deluge of last weekend converted the camp into a veritable quagmire. A most heavy down pour caused Cataracts and Waterfalls which made their appearance on the slopes and formed lakes in low-lying areas. One Orderly Room owes its escape from the flooding to the ingenuity of the regimental gardener. In laying out the grounds, he introduced an artificial bank in the scheme and this effectively dampened the rush of water, which reached a depth of two feet. Water and mud, however, have now become common place in our daily life, so that an increase in depth of a few inches does no longer alarm us, but rather affords the irrepressible jokers of whom there are many. One of the needle tounged 'Tommie's' on being asked the whereabouts of a certain Corporal replied "I don't know Sir, but I think he has gone on shore leave".

Caught up in the Kinmel Park Riot

Mary Evans

Mrs. Mary Evans recalled the day when soldiers went on the rampage. Mary went to work as usual as a cook at the Army Barracks at Kinmel. She normally helped out in the camp hospital kitchens, but on this particular day she was asked to assist in the bakery. A few hours into her working day, she heard a commotion outside. Men were shouting and she heard sounds of rifles being fired. The Kinmel Park Riot had begun, with Mary and innocent by-standers being caught up in the event.

Mrs. Evans who lived in Maes Conal in Abergele, at the time, stated she was not afraid. Soldiers were more involved in creating a fuss and fighting with men, rather than worrying about the civilian workers on the camp, especially the women. She was fortunate to be taken to a safe place by an unknown Canadian Sergeant Major.

One of Mary's sisters married a Sergeant Major from the camp. He, her brother in law, managed to get her a taxi, which returned her to Abergele. She did not return to the camp for a couple of days while things settled down.

Mrs. Evans was also working at the camp during the 'flu epidemic' which swept through the camp taking the lives of seventy eight service personnel.

Mary said she had to walk to and from work as there was no public transport at the time. Sadly, Mary was taken ill with pneumonia herself, and was off work for quite some time. She did not return to work at Kinmel Park Camp.

The Young Man who saw Five Soldiers die at Kinmel Park Camp

William Houlston

Mr. William (Bill) Houlston, just sixteen years old and an apprentice plumber who worked for the Balfour Beatty Company, stated: *"It was a tragedy and should never have happened. The Canadian soldiers smashed everything up due to not being paid"*. He also stated that "*At one time they had not been paid for three weeks, and that the tension built up to such a peak that the riot broke out. Bill watched the whole event from a safe distance, quoting about twenty Canadians started the whole thing, leading to all joining in, upon breaking into the wet canteens and warning the women to keep out of the way"*. No civilians were hurt during the rioting however, five soldiers were killed. Bill was one of a hundred men commissioned by the War Department to work on the camp. He worked at the camp until the end of the war. During the Second World War, Bill returned to Kinmel Park Camp, this time working for Martial Wards Building Contractors. Bill reported that the Second World War camp was only half the size of the First World War camp.

Canadian Soldier visits Kinmel Camp in 1968

Mr. Flemington

Mr. Flemington took time out of his visit to Great Britain to come and visit Kinmel Park Camp and the Canadian graves at St. Margaret's Church, Bodelwyddan. It was there, that a roommate was laid to rest, named Gunner Hickman. Hickman was shot through the heart; a stray shot came through the window of their billet killing him instantly. Mr. Flemington stated, *"They were sitting around the stove when a bullet came through the window and hit my friend, he was sitting right next to me"*. Sadly, Mr. Flemington said he could not find his friend's grave, as it had been snowing and that the snow had covered all the headstones.

The Flu Epidemic was a far Greater Tragedy

Eight graves of Royal Welsh Fusiliers, only just surpassed by the Royal Canadian Artillery (eleven graves). The Canadian Railway Troops (ten graves) and the 12th Reserve Battalion Canadian Infantry (nine graves). All died during the Flu Epidemic.

It is hard not to see how devastating this event was at Kinmel Park Camp. There were a total of eighty eight men and one woman who died in the seven months of the epidemic, between September 1918, and March 1919. On the 23rd September, 1918, alone, nine men died. There where formal military processions with gun carriages used to transport the coffins. The burials were made in a communal grave with the coffins being stacked three or four deep.

At a later date, all were exhumed and buried in individual plots. It should be noted that **Rebecca McIntosh**, a Nursing Sister, is buried at St. Margret's Church along with the men whom she cared for and eventually gave her life.

Rebecca was born on the 29th January 1892, into a farming family in Pleasant Bay, Nova Scotia. Her parents were **Peter and Christy McIntosh**. Her family included sisters **Margaret** and **Cassie**, and a brother, **John**. Her Grandmother **Annie,** also lived with the family. All the family were born in Canada except for Annie who was born in Scotland. Faith was a big part of Rebecca's early life. Her brother John was a Presbyterian Minister, and was named as her next of kin on her assetstation paper. (A form that all service personnel filled out on joining up). Many members of St. Matthews enlisted into the Armed Forces during the First World War, and sadly several lost their lives. This included a fellow Nursing Sister **Miss Pearle Frazer.** She was killed in action on His Majesties Hospital Ship 'Llandovery Castle'. Rebecca herself survived a very serious bout of scarlet fever in 1914. She recovered well enough to enlist into The Canadian Army Medical Corps at the age of twenty five.

On the 25th April, she sailed to England on HMHS 'Letitia'. This ship ran aground and sank on the return trip to Canada! Rebecca arrived in Liverpool just one week after leaving Canada. She was posted to the Kitchener Military Hospital (known later as No10 General) located in Brighton, Hampshire.

In the November of 1917, Rebecca was admitted to the KMH as a patient suffering from terrible abdominal pain. However, she was not operated on. She was diagnosed with acute appendicitis. It was apparent that her health was undermined by this illness, as well as the bout of Scarlet Fever she suffered back in Canada. Yet she did return to her duties on the wards. Rebecca was granted two leave periods while at KMH. Following her latest illness, she was posted to No9 (Canadian) General Hospital at Kinmel Camp, near Rhyl in North Wales. Kimnel Park Camp was a transit camp holding seventeen and a half thousand Canadian soldiers, awaiting repatriation back to Canada.

The winters in North Wales where miserable and very very cold. At the time there was a coal strike, so there was little fuel to heat the hospital. The food was poor.

The local shops overpriced their provisions. Tensions began to rise amongst the men. To compound this, the Spanish flu epidemic was sweeping through Europe; Kimnel Park Camp was not exempt to this.

An entry into No9 the Canadian general Hospital read:

'Influenza increasing rapidly in the Camp. The central part of the hospital is almost full. We have over six hundred patients in the hospital right now. Forty-nine were admitted yesterday and fifty-five today, practically all with influenza.'

The next day the writer of the dairy reported a further seventeen of this unit were in hospital. Nursing Sister Rebecca McIntosh would join them in mid February 1919. She struggled along with her illness; her breathing became more and more difficult. It was not a good time for her to be ill. The War Diary for the unit stated that Nursing Sister Rebecca McIntosh, eventually

sucumbed to her illness on the 8th March 1919. She was popular with her peers and the soldiers, regarded as a true Nursing Sister devoted to her duties. She is buried at St. Margaret's Church yard, Bodelwyddan, Flintshire, North Wales.

Florence May Currier

Staff Nurse Florence May Currier was posted to Kinmel Camp on the 17th February,1917. A report written about her competence stated *'she has worked at this hospital for eighteen months; she is a kind and willing nurse but lacks experience in ward management. She needs to work under supervision.'* She was posted to the British Expeditionary Force in France (No2 General Hospital) where she continued her duties until the July 1919.

Female Staff at Kinmel Decorated

Miss E St. Quintin

During February 1917, female members the Military Hospital staff were decorated for their War Service. This included Sister and Acting Matron **Miss E St. Quintin QAIMNS**. It was said that the hospital at Kinmel was a *'huge institution'*.

Miss Jean Roberts

Jean Roberts had joined the Women's Auxiliary Corps at Kinmel Park Camp. She was admitted to The Military Hospital in Bangor, N. Wales and died of an illness (spotted fever) in January 1916. Her mother was granted a pension after taking her case to Parliament.

Extracts from the Ontario Informer

George Timmins

Private 3235822 George Timmins of the 18th Battalion CEF, whose wife and three children lived in Albert Street, Oshawa, Ontario, had been overseas since the start of the Great War. This was sourced by a local paper in Oshawa Ontario Canada: *'He was wounded this past week by a gunshot to the hip'* (a shrapnel ball 8.5 cm smashed the left femur and he had two wounds in his right forearm). *It is hoped that these wounds are not serious ones.* On the 28th December, George was transferred to the 4th Canadian Reserve Battalion and on the 9th January, 1919, to Kinmel Park Camp near Rhyl in North Wales. George had got his 'Blighty'. (A wound that required him to return to Britain). He then returned to Canada onboard the 'Aquitania' on the 18th January, 1919, landing in Halifax on the 24th January.

John Dowe

Another soldier who had been at Kinmel Park Camp, was **Pri-**

vate John 'Jack' Dowe of the 123rd Pioneer Battalion. He had served at Passchendaele and Vimy Ridge before being sent to Kinmel Park Camp for repatriation to Canada. Whilst at Kinmel, John contacted a servere case of Influenza and did not fully recover until February 1919. He sailed back to Canada on 'The Empress of Britain' just prior to the Riots in March 1919. The old soldier that he was, Jack tried to join the Army again in 1939 but was deemed too old. Jack joined the Veterans Guard of Canada, guarding military in installations until war's end.

The Burlington Gazette –Ontario- Canada

Private Kerns

Private Kerns was born in Burlington, Ontario, a town just south of Milton. He was the son of Bruce Atkinson and Sarah Kerns of Zimmerman, Ontario. He attested into the 164th Battalion on 23rd March, 1916. He passed through the 2nd Reserve Training Battalion, prior to his service posting with the 102nd Battalion (4th Division, 11th Brigade) on the 28th February, 1918. On 24th October, Private Kerns was sent dangerously ill to the 33rd Casualty Clearing Station with suspected appendicitis. He had recently returned from Bourlon Wood, Canal du Nord and Cambria. (The 102nd Battalion being on loan to the 3rd Division).

He was subsequently sent to No8 Stationary Hospital, Wimereux, and then admitted to hospital in Manchester, England on the 26th October, 1918. where he received surgery. He was discharged 'fit for duty' to the 8th Reserve Battalion in Witley on the 31st January, 1919. Private Kerns was then admitted to No9 Canadian Hospital (Kinmel Camp) with severe abdominal Pains on 7th March, 1919. He died on the 9th March, 1919, after surgery to relive an intestinal obstruction. He is buried at St. Margaret's Church, Bodelwyddan, Flintshire, in North Wales.

Soldier Attempts to cut his Throat

A soldier only known as EJJ (Initials) who was at Kinmel Camp and who had not seen active service, was found unable to cope with the rigors of military training. EJJ was 19 years of age when he attempted to cut his throat. He was admitted to the Denbigh Asylum from the hospital at KPC. The only reason he could give for his attempted suicide was he was over worked in his training.

Private 49014 David Albert Evans

Private Evans the son of Enoch and Letitia Evans of Plain Dealings, Cilgerran Wales, worked as a gardener in Ireland before the war. He returned home to Wales in order to enlist into the army. He was posted to Kinmel Park Camp for his initial training as a Pte in the 3rd Battalion Welsh Regiment, the training battalion. This battalion supplied recruits to the Welsh Battalions at the front. David sadly became very ill with pneumonia whilst at Kinmel and died on the 14th February, 1917. His body was taken to Cilgerran and is buried at St. Lladdog Church yard. His coffin arrived draped in the Union flag. A large group of family and friends escorted him to his final resting place. He had two brothers. One brother James Samuel was killed in action while serving with the Black Watch, his other brother served in Salonika.

Private 25105 Francis Thomas

Above: Private Francis Thomas RWF (30)

Francis Thomas was born in Pentraeth, Anglesey 1884, Francis the son of Richard and Elizabeth Thomas (Richard was a farm Labourer) at Wigar Bach, Pentraeth. Francis also worked in agriculture prior to the Great War. He was married to Anne and had three children John, Richard and Margaret of 35, Wesley Street, Amlwch. Enlisting into the 17th Battalion Royal Welsh Fusiliers on the 2nd February, 1915, which formed part of the 38th Welsh Division. His initial training was at Kinmel Park Camp in North Wales. This Division landed in France in the December of 1915, before making their way into Flanders. They famously captured Mametz Wood along with other Welsh Battalions in early July 1916. On the morning of the 6th February, 1917, Thomas was in the reserve at Roussel Farm. The Battalion was asked to supply working parties engaged on railway construction, where he received serious wounds to the head, right arm and chest. He was taken to the 46th Casualty Clearing Station near Proven. This is where he sadly passed away due the seriousness of his wounds, He was 34 years old. Thomas is laid to rest at Mendinghem Military Cemetery. A Welshman through and through. The following is a poem written by Thomas's Grandson:

To a land where the white stones stand
Went the men from our fair land
To fight a war they didn't understand
To fight the Hun with grenade and gun
To die in the mud for the freedom of man
I went to see these men so brave
I went to see my Grandad's grave
So young were they to die this way
A Mother's son, a Father's pride
They should not have died
But while we remember that brave band
They are just resting in a foreign land
I went to see these men so brave
I went to see my Grandad's grave
Where the white stones stand.

Written by D Thomas

Above: Private 46132 William Ben Johnstone (31)

Ben Johnstone as he was known, was the fourth son of Benjamin and Johanna Johnstone. He was born 25th September, 1895, at Birkett Road, West Kirby. He enlisted into the army at Chester on the 9th December ,1915. He was 5' 9" tall and weighed 8st 13lbs. Ben was known to be in poor health and failed the medical for the Regiment of his choice the Cheshire Regiment. He decided to try elsewhere so that he could join his brothers serving at the front. Placed on the Reserve until 16th May, 1916, he became a Pte in the 12th Reserve Battalion RWF and commenced training a Kinmel Park Camp. On the 1st September, 1916, he embarked on the' HMS Franconia' to Davenport and arrived in Salonika. He was then transferred into the 11th Battalion.

**These events must have been heart breaking
for The Johnstone family (32)**

It reads as follows:

The receipt of a cablegram early this week by Mr. and Mrs. Ben Johnstone of 17 South Road, West Kirby (formerly of Grove Road) added another melancholy episode to the sad chapter of domestic happenings to which this family has endured since 1917. In four years Mr. and Mrs. Johnstone have lost five sons. Four of whom perished in the Great War. This week's sad news concerns Sydney who was 21 years of age, and sailed with the crew of the Lamport and Holt liner the Vasrai for South America. The ship had reached Buenos Ayres when Sydney Johnstone fell ill and died. Presumably he was laid to rest in that Southern City. Only the bare facts have reached his sorrowing parents, but he had a pal on board with him (Horace Roberts of Grange Road, West Kirby). Who will it is believed, be able to relate the exact circumstances later. **Sydney Johnstone** was passionately fond of the sea. During the war, he had a terrible experience whilst afloat. He was aboard the 'Justicia' when that fine vessel was sent to the bottom by a U Boat torpedo in 1918. He received a severe shock but escaped with his life, losing all else that he possessed and suffering many hours exposure in a small boat. Of the other son's, Private William Johnstone made the great sacrifice on June 28th, 1917. At the age of twenty seven. On the following day, his brother **Joseph Johnstone** laid down his life at the age of thirty one. Then, **Private Ernest Johnson** fell in action in France in June 1918, at the age of twenty. **Private Benjamin Johnstone** died at the Edinburgh War Hospital, on January 31st, 1919. The life of Private William Johnston was spared, but he was unfortunate enough to have both his feet amputated through accidently getting them under a troop train in France.

Above: the Hospital Ship St Andrews (33)

Frank Thorley MM

Lcpl 59980 Frank Thorley MM was born in Manchester, England 16th January, 1896. He attested into the 21st Battalion CEF at Kingston, Ontario. He embarked for Southampton, England on 6th May, 1915, on board 'RMS Metagama', disembarking 15th May, 1915, proceeding to West Sandling Camp near Hythe in Kent. Thorley arrived in Boulogne, France on 15th September, 1915. On 8th April, 1916, he received wounds at St. Eloi to his thigh, arms, chest and buttocks. He was admitted to the Canadian Field Hospital at Dickiebusch, then sent to the Causality Clearing Station at Bailluel, moving to No4 General Hospital in Camiers.

Eventually, he was invalided back to the UK on board the Hospital Ship 'St. Andrews' on 12th April, 1916. He was later admitted to the Duchess of Connaught Red Cross Hospital, at Taplow, in Buckinghamshire. He stayed at various Military Hospitals and establishments in the UK between 14th May and 13th October, 1916. On 19th December, 1916, he was posted to the Canadian Composite Training Battalion at Shoreham in Kent eventually being posted back to the 21st battalion in France on 6th March, 1917. He was promoted to Lance Corporal on 19th May, 1917. On 21st November, 1917, the 21st Battalion were involved in heavy fighting at Crest farm and for his courage that day, he was recommended for the Military Medal. On 5th December, 1917, in the 2nd Division Routine Orders, it announced the award of the MM to Thorley and nine other men from the 21st Battalion. Thorley was promoted to Corporal on 1st February, 1919, and posted to Kinmel Park Camp Military District 3 in North Wales, pending his repatriation back to Canada. He was moved about quite a bit with the Military Districts during his stay. At one time he was attached to the Commonwealth War Graves Commission from 25th March until 2nd July, 1919. On July 5th, he sailed from Liverpool to Canada on board RMS 'Carmania'.

Thorley, was a very brave man as is evident below:

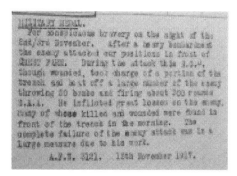

Citation for Thorley MM (34)

'Military Medal. For conspicuous bravery on the night of the 2nd/3rd November. After a bombardment the enemy attacked our positions in front of Crest farm. During the attack this NCO though wounded, took charge of a portion of the trench and beat off a large number of the enemy throwing 50 bombs and firing 300 rounds S.A.A. He inflicted great losses on the enemy, many of those killed and wounded were found in front of the trench in the morning. The complete failure of the enemy attack was in large measure due to his work. A.F.W 3121 dated 15th November, 1917.

Chaplin General

Kinmel Park Camp received a visit from **Chaplin General Bishop Taylor** on the 16th June, 1917.

The Duchess of Westminster

The Duchess visited Kinmel Park Camp on the 13th April, 1918 to open a new portion of the YMCA in Camp four.

The Toronto Star 8th March 1919

The riot at Rhyl was the second affair of its kind in which Canadian soldiers overseas had been involved since the Armistice was signed. But it must be very trying to be all ready to sail and then have the sailing cancelled. The trouble amongst the Canadians at Rhyl is largely due to the cancelling of sailings. The 'Olympic' after four years on the Canadian run, needs a more convincing explanation than any yet given. It carried Canadians to War and is now carrying Americans home.

This letter appears in the London Times, addressed to the Editor of the Times, written on the 10th March, 1919. "Sir, as one who is closely associated with and a near neighbor of Kinmel Park Camp I venture to ask you to grant me space for a brief statement on what recently happened".

"I desire to keep as distinct as may be possible, the causes in this particular outbreak and the question of the discipline of the Canadians in this camp". Kinmel last autumn was assigned to the Canadians, and for three months has been for them a demobilization camp. More than forty thousand men have already passed through. Discomforts in the camp thus perpetually changing are inevitable. The General and his staff did their best to remove discomforts when the men complained that coal was scarce, that the huts were cold, that the floors were too drafty to sleep upon and blankets were scant, also adding to the list that their food was not very appetizing. These things have been borne with patience. But cancellations of sailing coming week after week to war-torn men yearning for home, have been a very serious matter. A man arrives at Kinmel, having been told that he is to sail in a few days for Canada and having received his last pay certificate. Weeks passed and he is still there. He may have been in the fighting line, and sees that those who had little or no fighting allowed to sail before him. Thus the fire began to smolder. It burst into flames when in the illustrated Canadian newspapers, the men saw the acclaimed arrival of conscripts who had done little or no fighting.

One said to me, it is a bit hard that these fellows should have all the home cheers.

Whether the fire was fanned into flames by Russians or aliens, I know not: my only aim is to give as fully and fairly as I can the whole circumstances. I have seen a good deal of camps by virtue of my position during the war. I have no desire to palliate what happened at Kinmel. But I do not know whether Englishmen would have borne similar conditions without protest. I am certain Welshmen would not. As to the behavior and character of the men at Kinmel Camp, I can speak with personal knowledge. Those in charge of the canteens which I know very well, speak in high praise of the conduct of the men. The Superintendent of the largest hut in the camp the 'YMCA' speaks with long experience, week after week reports to me the admirable conduct of the men who throng to this hut. The ladies resident in this neighborhood opened of their own accord a canteen for the Canadians who crowd into our village to use it. Amid the hundreds that each day visit the canteen there has been not one single incident of rudeness or roughness. We in this countryside are indeed proud to have amongst us those men who have fought so gallantly for their Motherland.

Your Obedient Servant. A G Asaph.

Dr. Howard Clouston

The following is an extract of a letter written by **Doctor Captain Howard Clouston CAMC,** to his mother on the subject of the Kinmel Camp riots, written from No 8 :

"Briefly, the facts are that men were sore because the 3rd Division were getting the boats. The 3rd was going home in complete units. Now a lot of the original units are here and their places were filled by conscripts when they were wounded etc. Therefore draftees were getting home as the 'originals' and the real 'originals' were staying here. Headed by a few fools, they started at their own canteens and got to eat and drink some beer. I was up until 3am patching up a couple of bruised heads. When daylight came the looting continued and they got a couple of railcars loaded with beer, on the track right here in the camp. They did not fire on the officer's quarters, there were no officer's, Victoria Cross or others killed, although a few received some stone wounds, etc. Five of the rioters are dead, two are danger-

ously ill and about thirty men are in hospital. We were fairly busy of course with others who had minor injuries. The rioters did rob the Sergeant's Messes and the Officer's Messes of their booze, as well as their own wet canteens, but only smashed their own living quarters and some of the guard rooms. They appropriated all the tobacco and emptied the central canteen stores. They also took all the stores from the Quartermaster stores, also looting and smashing the YMCA, but not the Salvation Army. They were absolutely insane in the way they went for their own quarters and yet left ours alone. They did smash up 'Tin Town"'and the stores of the civilians here on the camp. There was a small amount of stray shooting, mostly by drunken soldiers. In fact it was the booze that did the whole thing. General Turner VC, KCB, came up from London by train, not by airplane. The news reports where written in Rhyl and were very incorrect. At Rhyl they were very frightened by events. Of course, five dead is bad enough and a few thousand dollars damage pretty expensive. There is a notion that there is something behind it all. One Russian leader was killed, he got a bayonet through the stomach, and another Russian is in jail and maybe shot! They have all sorts of evidence against him. The General addressed the men in fifteen different places within the confines of the camp. I am sorry to spoil some good newspaper stories, but I know the facts. Your son, Howard".

Note: Dr. Clouston was incorrect in this statement as Private Gillan was not one of the rioters. He was defending the camp against the rioters. He was shot in the back by one of his own peers.

Published in the Huntingdon Gleamer on the 27th March, 1919.

A Long way to go, and not get to the Front

Charles Best

Private Charles Best of Camp Petawawa, Ontario, was drafted for France on the 5th September, 1918, which turned out to be cancelled, but he managed to sail on the 18th October for England, as part of a draft for the 2nd Canadian Tank Battalion, sailing on the transport ship 'Victoria'. Whilst on board, Charles was promoted to Sergeant in charge of one hundred men. The voyage took seventeen days (normally a five day trip). During the crossing, nine men lost their lives to influenza and where buried at sea. The Victoria had no doctors or nurses onboard. Charles said he survived by taking mast duties and sleeping on the deck. His destination was Kinmel Park Camp in N. Wales. Once at Kinmel he said Infantry drill kept the men occupied and they went on long foot marches to the foothills of Mount Snowdon, as the authorities needed to keep the men busy and out of trouble. Charles was promoted to Acting Sergeant Major, as his friend (the Company Sergeant Major) had become ill with Influenza. With the Armistice, discipline evaporated. Best and a Sergeant friend of his, hired a car for a week and toured the South of England. While in London, they wore civilian overcoats to hide their uniforms. They borrowed two officer's caps and enjoyed being saluted. On their return trip to KPC they toured up through Wales. They went to a show in Rhyl to see a Welsh Male Voice Choir perform. *"The best voices I have ever heard"*, commented Charlie. Charlie did not get to see France but like many young soldiers wished he had. He did witness the Kinmel Park Riots stating that *"tempers were very high and we found ourselves in the midst of some vicious skirmishes"*. Best's unit arrived back in Canada in December of 1919, sailing on the 'Aquitania' from Southampton.

They Remained in the United Kingdom

At the end of World War One, **15,182** Canadian servicemen signed away their right to free transportation home to Canada. They wished to remain in the United Kingdom. Added to this number were **7,136** men who had been discharged before the Armistice. They also wished to stay, it meant that **22,000** Canadians entered civilian life in the UK. No doubt many where of British decent.

Canadian Soldier Private Robert J Ritchie

On Thursday 12th December, 1918, **Private Robert J Ritchie** of Kinmel Camp, was charged with stealing beer. It was alleged that he had stolen beer from casks from the railway track at Kinmel. Ritchie admitted to having taken the beer however, he contended, it was handed it to him by another man. He was found guilty and committed to one month in prison. He immediately gave notice of appeal against his sentence. The Magistrates released him on bail in order for Ritchie to get legal assistance. On Monday 16th December,1918. Rhyl Magistrates were informed that Ritchie had decided not to proceed further with his appeal, and surrendered himself to the authorities.

Note: It is unknown the outcome of these events.

Number 2 Construction Battalion CEF

Above: The cap badge of the No2 Construction Battalion (35)

A most severe incident of racial antagonism occurred after the Great War. When this Construction Battalion returned to Great Britain, Kinmel Park Camp, where it awaited repatriation to

Canada, like many parts of the Canadian Expeditionary Forces during this time. On the 7th January, 1919. Some two hundred and seventy-five men of the company were involved in a melee with fellow Canadian soldiers. The incident occurred after **Sergeant Edward Sealy** of No2CB, ordered a white JNCO to be locked up, because he allegedly refused to take an order from Sealy, whilst making racist remarks. Members of the white JNCO's unit took exception to the fact that a black man had arrested a white soldier, and decided to confront the Construction Company while it was on parade. A small riot ensued, and a number of men from both sides were slashed with razors and beaten with rocks. Many of the No2CB huts had their windows smashed. At the time of the incident, **Sir Edward Kemp**, The Minister for Overseas Military Forces for Canada, was ignorant to the fact that this unique formation existed. Sir Edward told fellow **MP Jacques Bureau** (Member of Parliament for Trios-Riveres) that *"If 'Negros' were in the Canadian Army at all, they were scattered throughout the Forces"*.

Note: the No2 Construction Company was raised in Nova Scotia, and was a predominantly made up of black men. It was commanded by **Lt. Col D. H Sutherland**. The unit was formerly known as the 193rd Battalion CEF. All the officers serving where white within the officer corps, with the exemption of one black officer, which was **Captain William A White** the unit Chaplin.

Above: Members of a Canadian Construction Unit (36)

Some of the Private Soldiers who served in No2 Construction Company:

Private 931335 Clarence Allison, Private Kenneth 931053 Allison, Private 931358 Walter R Allison, Private 931206 William Allison, Private 931163 George W Bushford, Private 931103 Harold F Bushford, 931149 Philip A Bushford, Private 931156 Robert J Bushford, Private 931501 Henry F Courtney, Private 931345 Garret W Cox, Private 931317 Charles J Cromwell, Private 931312 James A Cromwell, Private 931315 Joseph H Cromwell, Private 931314 Joseph O Cromwell. Private 931302 Neilly Cromwell, Private 931405 Ethelbert L Cross, Private 931226 Clifford W Downey, Private 931089 Frederick G Elms, Private 931092 Walter H Elms, Private 931156 Harmon E. Farmer, Private 931248 Thomas Goffigan, Private 931072 John W Hamilton, Private 931386 Garfield Parris, Private 931004 James Parris, Private 931017 James A Parris, Private 931307 William W Parris. Private 931805 Wallace J. Pleasant, Private 931114 Percy J Richards, Private 931946 James A Talbot, Private 931047 James I Talbot, Private 93117 Percy W Thomas, Private 931389 George W Tolliver, Private 931003 William Tolliver, Private 931239 Arthur S Tyler, Private 931657 Arthur Nelson Ware, Private 931555 Benjamin Washington, Private 931613 Robert C Whims, Private 931229 Charles G Wilson. Many more men served with the Company.

Kinmel Camp Billets sold

At the end of the war, some of the buildings at Kinmel Park were sold. One building was sold to **Mr. Owen Roberts** of Maesgwyn. Mr. Roberts used the building he purchased as a holiday cottage. It has the signatures of a number of New Brunswicker's scratched into the inside of the wooden door , they are there to this day. One particular building was sold to the town of St. Asaph, and was used as their community hall. The front of the building still stands to this day. A personal friend of mine has Canadian Pine holding up his roof here in Colwyn Bay, purchased from Kinmel Camp, some 30 years ago, when he was building his new home.

Lieutenant Commander Hermann Tholens
The Daily Post (extracts from the newspaper report)

In August of 1915, three German POW's escaped from Kinmel Park Camp Bodelwyddan, or so at the time it was believed. The three men headed for Llandudno, when a chance meeting occurred between a local lady and Lieutenant Commander Tholens. While walking along a street in the town, Tholens stopped a young lady who was taking her daughter for a walk in her pram. He complimented **Mrs. Laura Jane Jones** on her beautiful daughter whilst reaching down and depositing his Eiserne Kreuz 2nd Klasse (Iron Cross 2nd Class) into the pram. Later that day, he handed himself over to a local police officer, **Morris Williams** outside the Tudno public house, as their plan to meet up with the submarine had failed. They tried for three days to meet up with the subs, failing because they were in the wrong place, mainly due to a rocky out crop on the beach they were signalling from. '*So near yet so far*'''as they say. The Germans were heading for the Great Orme where they were to rendezvous with U-38 and U27 of the German Navy. The three Germans were recaptured. The other two Germans with Tholens were **Captain Heinrich von Hennig** and **Captain Wolf Dietrich Baron von Helldorf.** They gave themselves up trying to get to London. The medal has since been returned to a family member of Lt. Cmdr Hermann Tholens. Tholens was the second in command of the 'Cruiser Mainz' which was sunk off the coast of Northern Germany, where he was taken prisoner. He was repatriated from Switzerland to Germany in 1919, and died in 1967.

Note: On further investigation into this gentleman and his fellow officers, they were also said to have escaped from 'Pyffry Aled POW Camp' near Llansannan in N. Wales, the latter POW camp being correct camp from which these three escaped.

**Above: Lieutenant Commander Hermann Tholens
captured in Llandudno, in this picture he is in the
long coat second to the left (37)**

Irving Henry Jones

Sourced from the Flintshire Archives.

Irving was aged just 16 when he enlisted into the army. He presented himself as being 21 years of age, born in Bedwas, S. Wales. He initially went to the town of Rhyl. Kinmel Camp was still under construction. He paraded in civilian buttoned boots, a suit and a boater hat. No uniforms were issued as there were none to be given at that time. Rifle drill was with wooden pales. Later during their training, they were given a wooden rifle before they eventually received the real thing. Whilst in training, his unit the Welsh Regiment, were given the once over by experts looking for underage recruits. Young Jones thrust his chin out to the inspecting officer, he shaved twice a day and managed to pull the wool over the experts. On one occassion the whole unit went on strike (well the majority were miners). They had been promised leave, but were given none. On one particular morning the Regiment paraded with a bugle call for them to fall in, this being ignored to a man. Leaders were chosen from within the ranks of the men to talk with the officers about the leave problem. This produced the desired effect and leave was granted to the men. During his stay in Rhyl, young Jones was billeted at 6, Gronant Ave, where he was taken in as one of their own. He qualified as a signalman, and he and the Welsh Regiment left for France. The locals of Rhyl gave the Battalion a most affectionate send-off, with gifts to the men and their sincere best wishes ringing in their ears. In the September 1915, they embarked for France and Irving remembers being very, very ill on the trip across the English Channel, and wishing he was dead. He survived the Great War.

**Above: The 38th Brigade (The Welsh Division)
Memorial at Memetz Wood (38)**

Fred Rowlands

Fred was born in Welshpool, but he moved to S. Wales in search of work down the pit. He became a timberman at Blaengarw Pit, joining the army with the Cardiff Pals Battalion – the Welsh Regiment, just one month after war was declared. Fred was living in the village of Pontycymmer. He had a wife and baby daughter. His initial training commenced at Colwyn Bay, in N. Wales I think he was in billets there and waiting for Kinmel Park Camp to be built. The Regiment had men in billets along the coast near to the Camp. They were part of the newly formed 30th Brigade of the Welsh Division, the brain child of **Lloyd George**. Once his training was complete, Fred and his Regiment proceeded to France in the September of 1915. By the June of

1916, Fred was a Lance Corporal. He was to play his part in the battle of Memetz Wood on the 7th July, 1916. The Battle of the Somme, as it became known, was just one week old. Fred led his platoon and in their attack they were caught up in a murderous cross fire, along with the South Wales Borderers', on their flank. It was commented upon that no men could have taken their objective that day as there were German machine guns to their front and to their side. His Battalion attacked three times that day, and in one of the attacks, Fred fell mortally wounded. The Battalion lost over 400 men during these attacks.

Note: Over five days, the 38th Brigade lost more than 4,000 men, most of them killed trying to take the wood. The Towns and Villages the length and breadth of Wales were cast into great morning. A sad time indeed. I once gave a historical tutorial on Memetz Wood at Wrexham Museum. There was not a dry eye in the house. These men were wrongly accused of being poorly trained and cowards, by their Generals. However, after the battle, many awards and citations for bravery to these men counteracted the statement of poorly trained and cowards. The Generals had to eat their words.

Above: The Death Penny of Private Fred Rowlands of the Welsh Regiment (39)

Above: Postcard – the Last Bus (40)

One can only imagine this bus also being filled with young soliders, escaping the confines of Kinmel Park Camp at every opportunity. Heading to places like Rhyl, Abegele, Colwyn Bay and even Llandudno.

Above: St. Margarets Church cica 1920 (41)

Note: The white wooden crosses scattered all over the church yard, nowdays they all stand side by side in neat rows and are made of sandstone.

Sgt 13575 Leonard (John) Nuttall – The Welsh Regiment

Sgt Nuttall went by the name of John whilst serving with the 9th Welsh Regiment, where he suffered a serious wound to his head. On recovery, he was posted to Kinmel Park Camp, with the 12th Regiment, a training Battalion. John was one of the training cardre only for a matter of weeks before taking his own life. The deputy coroner for Flintshire (at St. Asaph) reported it was a very sad case of suicide. He was found by a passer by in some fields near Bryn Elwy, who stated that he noticed a soldier apparently standing under a tree. On getting closer he found the soldier was suspended from the tree by a rope. His feet being approximatley 2 feet from the ground. He was cut down, but life was extinct. On the ground near to the body was the Sergents cap containing a hand written note. John was 34 years old and was unmarried. Prior to the outbreak of war, he was employed as a colliery check weigh-man in South Wales. He joined the army within a month of the outbreak of hostilities, and went to the front as part of the 9th Welsh Regiment. He took part in all the Regiments campaigns up until he received his wound.

John's final letter read: *'D Coy Welsh Regiment, Kinmel Camp. Can not rest day or night my head hurts so bad. I am grieving to think of the pain and trouble it'll cause, but I am going to seek the other world. May God comfort my dear ones and have mercy on my soul. I am better dead than insane, and I have done my bit for England. Goodbye all'.*

Another letter was also produced to the Coroner. It reads to his Officer Commanding, *'A request that he should be allowed to revert back to the rank of private on account of his memory and weak nerves, due to shock. Sgt Nuttalls regimental conduct sheet was produced to the court. He had a clean record. A verdict of suicide whilst temorarily insane was recorded in this case'.*

Fletcher F

Private 59532 Fletcher joined the 53rd Young Soldier Battalion (The Liverpool Regiment, formely 72nd Young Soldier Battalion – 21st battalion The Lancashire Fusiliers), and was sent for initail training at Kinmel Park Camp on 27th October. He was billeted in D Company lines of Camp 17.

Letter to the The Prime Minster of Canada

A letter written to **Sir Robert Borden** (PM of Canada) questioning the legitimacy of the General Courts Martial (Kinmel Park Camp Riots, June 1919). **Captain G Black** a Barrister and officer in the Canadian Machine Gun Corps. Black was part of the defence of the British Columbian soldiers involved in the riots. *'The GCM being held in Liverpool in the June of 1919. Black questioned the propiety and legitimancy of the proceedings were he requested to have thirty men in prison in Great Britain be released. He also stated comments and circustances of the riot and the terrible conditions at KPC. Black also enclosed a sealed letter reiterating his own anxity that the injustices of the trials had still not be undone'.*

Also enclosed, extracts of a letter written in the April of 1919. The letter was written by **Private C. E Sparrow**, where he described *'his disaffection and of the low moral at the camp from the continued delays in the Canadains repartriation'.*

Captian William George Bartholomew

Captain Bartholomew of the 48th Highlanders of Canada (134th Battalion CEF), was present during the riots at the camp. He watched with interest as two Canadain Soliders approched a British General with two pails of ale. They laid them before him and smartly saluted . The General saluted back and spoke to them briefly before he continued on his way. Captain Bartholomew further stated that there were about **5,000** involved in the riots. He returned to Canada under first class conditions, when finally he arrived home, there was no home coming reception for the ship he was on. I think this was a sad state of affairs.

Between the Wars

The Kings Own Royal Regiment

Sometime in the spring of 1933, the Kings Own Royal Regiment took up training at Kinmel Camp. I found it odd that with all the accommodation they were under canvas.

Above: Three members of the Kings

Own Royal Regiment KPC. Sometime during 1933 (42)

Above: some officers at rest in the field (43)

An Artillery Unit under canvas at Kinmel (44)

Chapter 9

1939-45 KINMEL PARK CAMP

Not much can be found on the activities about the camp during the Second World War. 'As Careless Talk Costs Lives' (as quoted by Churchill) was the order of the day. This was certainly prevalent at Kinmel Park Camp. I have sourced the local newspapers only to find snippets of the goings on there; these are documented within these pages.

In the September of 1939, in the Rhyl Journal, it was reported that a concert was held at the camp at the YMCA, which was a great success. This was the second concert held during that time, and more were planned. Oddly enough, there was no mention of any more concerts for the duration of the war within its pages.

Notes were as follows:-

> *'It would not surprise me, the writer, in the least to hear 'the powers that be' have sent a compliment to the YMCA.* **Mrs. Stone** *should have realized that no building in the camp can stand such vociferous applause without the roof falling in. The writer was at a show only last week and cannot remember ever having attended one at which the audience was so appreciative.*
>
> *Note: There was no room for late comers.*

The following service personnel must be congratulated for their contribution. **Private Tom Jones** *- On the Piano,* **Private Cornell** *- Recitation,* **Private Richards** *– Singer,* **Lance Corporal D. O Davies** *– singing of 'The Famers Boy',* **Bandsman Smith** *– Singer,* **Private Bendall** *Comic/Humorist,* **Private Llewelyn Williams** *– Singing of 'Irish Eyes',* **Corporal James, Private Roy, Private Lambert** *and* **Miss Krietmair** *– Singing Group.*

Various occurrences happened at the camp which made it into the Journal over the next 5 years. I have collated them in order of presidency.

Various News Paper Articles - Rhyl
Painter Falls to his Death

Cyril A Felton

*During some refurbishment work on the camp, a civilian workman (a painter) fell to his death in the September of 1939. The painter was working on accommodation buildings, when a plank broke causing **Mr. Cyril A Felton** of Middlesex, to fall, thus causing his death.*

Plumber Accused of Theft
Samuel O'Brien

Mr. Samuel O' Brien, *a Rhyl man was charged with stealing copper piping from Kinmel Park Camp. Valued at three shillings and nine pence, the property of the War Office. He appeared in Court on the 10th October, 1939. O'Brien was fined ten shillings. It was noted at the time 'that anyone else caught stealing from the Camp will be seriously dealt with', so said the Chairman of the Bench.*

Labour at Kinmel Camp

In the July of 1939, it was believed that one hundred and seventy eight men had been employed as carpenters at Kinmel Camp. These men had come from Southern Ireland. They were said to be fully trained in this skill. However, it was later to be found not true. Local men of excellent character were said to be anxious to take up these positions, and certainly made their feeling known.

One wonders how this matter was resolved!

Petty Theft of Cigarettes and Matches
Robert Haworth and William Heap

*Two Soldiers, **Private's Robert Haworth** and **William Heap** were* *handed over to the Provost of Kinmel Park Camp, by local police. The soldiers were arrested by police for stealing matches and cigarettes from West Parade, Rhyl. The handing over of petty criminals/service personnel was to become the normal practice for the duration. (A Home Office Edict).*

Theft of Chocolate
Ernst Pimm

Gunner Ernst Pimm, stole chocolate from a machine at Rhyl Railway Station. Pimm was sentenced to two months hard labor for this offence.

Theft of Army Rations
James Ellison

Two months hard labour for a cook working at Kinmel Park Camp. Mr. James Ellison of Liverpool, did steal two tins of milk, two pounds of butter, six and half pounds of sugar, three pounds of tea to the value of thirteen shillings, reported by the Camp Messing Officer, Lieutenant Edward Wilson.

Second Class Citizens – Intruders

It was noted that soldiers from Kinmel Park Camp were looked upon by the people of Rhyl as 'intruders'. This was reported by Captain H.A Parry the Camp Padre.

I guess nothing changes!

Hard Swearing in St. Asaph
William Woods and Frank Stapleton

Gunners William Woods and Frank Stapleton, who were fast asleep in their billets, or were they? A case of off camp without permission of the military. It was reported that both servicemen were seen riding their bikes around the town of St. Asaph.

Gunner 151320 Woods, Gunner 1493118 Stapleton. Lieutenant R.S Fitch made a statement to police that " were absent from camp and not in their billets", as they stated to Police. They were found guilty of causing a nuisance. Stapleton was fined ten shillings and Woods five shillings.

It did not stop there as both men would have been subject to Military Law to compound their punishment.

Soldier Found Shot in Rhyl Train
Frank Newcome

Gunner Frank Newcome accidently shot himself when he was getting ready to alight a train at Rhyl Station. He was taken to the War Memorial Hospital. Newcome made a full recovery.

Bigamy by Soldier
Robert S Cook

Sergeant Robert Sidney Cook, Royal Artillery, appeared before the Chair Mr. P J Ashfield CBE on a charge of bigamy, in that he married a Miss Adelaide Humphreys at St. Asaph on 27th June, 1940. When already married to Emma May Cook of Bisley, Surrey.

Fatal Collison at Kinmel Bay
Joseph Spencer

Gunner Joseph Spencer aged 24 was travelling on St. Asaph Ave in the direction of Bodelwyddan, when a collision occurred with a motor vehicle. Spencer died at the scene of the acciden,t while Gunner Alfred Wright was injured, he being the pillion passenger of the motor cycle.

Soldier Killed near Rhuddlan
Charles Molineux

Gunner Charles Molineux was killed by a motor vehiclewhen walking to Rhuddlan from Kinmel Park Camp. He was 20 years old. Three friends he was walking with at the time of the accident were uninjured.

Soldier Found shot and Poisoned
Robert Cutler

*A tragic event happened at Kinmel Park Camp, when **Gunner Robert Cutler** was found to have shot himself in the head. He was found in his billets ablutions. It is believed that he also used ammonia to assist in the act of suicide. Gunner Cutler had been in the Army just six weeks.*

Soldier Stole Postal Order
James Edward Warren

*__Gunner James Edward Warren__ aged 17, was accused of stealing a Postal Order worth ten shilling. The property of **Gunner John Meader**. The offence occurred between 1st and 16th August, 1940. Warren was fined fifteen shilling (court costs) and ordered to pay Meader ten shilling in respect of the Postal Order.*

Petrol Theft Charges Against Soldiers
Arthur A. E Willis and George A Unsworth

*__Company Quarter Master Sergeant Arthur Edwin Joseph Willis__ and **Driver George A. Unsworth** were charged with stealing six gallons of petrol valued at twelve shillings, the property of the War Department (4th December,1940). The Soldiers were caught red handed cross loading the fuel into a taxi cab in Rhyl. Sentence being deferred to the Military.*

Stole cash and property of Mr. Stephens
James Kinsella and Lawrence Moisiechik

Two soldiers, **Fusilier's James Kinsella** and **Lawrence Moisiechik** 19 and 17 respectfully, stole cigarettes, chocolate and money to the value of six pounds, one shilling and seven pence, the property of **Richard Stephens** of the Okenhurst Cafe Rhyl.

The excuse given by the servicemen was that Mr. Stephens over charged them on their credit bill. It was noted that both had only been in the army a few weeks. They were given one month hard labour. The Commanding Officer stated, that he did not want to "*keep the defendants in the army under any circumstances as they were liable to contaminate decent young fellows in it*".

Officers Failure to Immobilize Motor Vehicle
Stephen H Cox

Lieutenant Stephen H Cox, was charged with failing to immobilize his vehicle, in Sussex Street, Rhyl, at 1100 hours on the 14th January, 1941. The officer stated that "*it was an oversight after setting down some soldiers after giving them a lift into Rhyl*". A fine of ten shilling was imposed for the offence.

Charges against a Soldier and a Silk Worker
Bertrand Ives

Theft of army clothing in wholesale fashion from Kinmel Park Camp by **Sergeant Bertrand Ives** *(Royal Corps of Signals) to the value of seven pounds, on the 13th February, 1941. Over time, two hundred pounds worth of military clothing had been spirited away. Sold to* **Mr. Charles Oswald Leonard Dicken**. *A courts martial was held at Kinmel Park Camp with wholesale charges being laid against a number of Non Commissioned Offices. They were all charged with theft, following on from the initial charge held against Sergeant Ives. Two more service men were charged with theft offences. They were* **Company Quarter Master Sergeant Walter Upton** *and* **Corporal (Acting Sergeant) John B Ives**. *It was stated that if ever a case should be made public it was this one. Both servicemen worked at the Camp Stores at Kinmel Park. The charges for the theft of boots, socks, vests, trousers, and other articles, the property of the War Department.*

Note: That **Mr. Dicken** was given a 4 month custodial sentence for receiving stolen goods by the civilian court. The courts martial continued against the servicemen.

Army Sports – A successful Athletic Meet was held in N. Wales.

*The first of what is to be a series of Annual Athletic Meets, will be held at The Anti-Aircraft Driver Training Regiment, Kinmel Park Camp, by the kind **Lt. Colonel D. C Wilson**, of the Royal Artillery. The meet was well attended and splendidly organized with all events being keenly contested. There was even a musical ride given by a display team under the direction of **Lieutenant. J Foss** Royal Artillery. This event gave the crowd an imminence thrill, which was followed by a gymnastics display, given by the Army Physical Training Corps staff, under the instruction of **Company Sergeant Major Instructor C.E Franklin**.*

Admin Battery played A Battery at sack football and push ball. These events provoked the crowd into roars of laughter. The tug of war final was grimly fought out, with B Battery being declared winners. What a wonderful day was had by all who partook and spectated.

Soldier Deprived of Choice of Trial by Jury. The Rhyl Journal 7ᵗʰ September, 1942
Thomas Glazsbrook

*Gunner Thomas Glazsbrook Jones, Royal Artillery aged 32, under training at Kinmel Park Camp for just one month was charged with attempted shop breaking and alternately attempting to steal a gold watch, the property of **Mr. John H Lipman**, Jewelers of Rhyl. Valued nine pounds five shilling. During the early hours of Sunday morning, Jones was handed over to a Military Escort he was taken to Kinmel Park Camp for further action against him.*

Theft Charge Fails
Thomas E Carmichael

A strongly suspected soldier was slapped in the face after trial. (A young woman's shattered romance).

The Court witnessed a dramatic climax on Friday, after the case against **Lance Bombardier Thomas E. Carmichael** *of Kinmel Park Camp for the theft of a bag, containing sixteen pounds, ten shilling and eight pence. The property of Eldorado Ice Cream Company at the Lyons Camp, Rhyl.*

Football Friendly.

Search Light TC Regiment played the Military College of Science in a pre-season friendly, with the Search Light TC Regiment coming out on top by a score of 9 - 2. Both teams are due to meet again in League Football. A keen rivalry was evident shortly after kick off. The Search Light side got into their stride keeping the visitors defense alert by a fast clever forward line, supported by their half backs. Military College of Science gave a good account of themselves. Eventually being beaten. The outstanding players on the day were **Pilling, Watmore** *and* **Shaw** *for the SL side and Murray, Crowe and Webb for the MCS side. Note: that this coming Saturday MCS will be playing the 11th Anti-Aircraft Training Regt, KPC at Belle Vue, Grange Rd, Rhyl. Kick Off 1500 hours.*

YMCA – Kinmel Park Camp sells bread to soldier William H Stratton

The sale of bread contravening the bread Order, to **Gunner William Henry Stratton** *without a license granted by the Ministry, and at a price exceeding the current price under the order (Note: the cost of a loaf of bread being six pence ,or one penny per slice, one and half pence buttered, all food stuffs must be eaten on the property). Gunner Stratton purchased bread and took it off the YMCA premises, taking it to the guardroom for the guard to consume. The Judge made a comment to the petty session's court that this case was a total waste of the courts time.*

Kinmel Park Camp Sport.

All types of sports were taken seriously at Kinmel during WW2, especially football. Sport was the great de-stressor of the day. Sport continued to be a big part of the camps life way into the future.

A Soldier Carefully Calculated Fraud against the Railway. (Unnamed)

A soldier was fined one pound and ordered to pay one pound costs for travelling on the railway without a ticket on 16th November, 1942. He was not named. The Judge stated because the soldier was experiencing domestic problems at home, his judgment would be lenient in this case. It is to be noted that this was the first offence committed by a service man in over a year.

Soldiers Committed for Trial
Norman K Baxter and Charles W Brant

Two soldiers Gunners Norman K Baxter and Charles W Brant, alleged to have stolen cigarettes and tobacco from the Erias Park Cafe, Colwyn Bay on the night of 14/15th July, 1943. The amount stolen was to the value of twelve pounds, fifteen shilling and one and a half pence. The soldiers were committed for trail.

Military Wedding - Constance Ruth Williams and Thomas Laing

Private Constance Ruth Williams (ATS) and **Sergeant Thomas Laing** (Anti-Tank Regiment RA, Kinmel Park Camp) were married at the English Presbyterian Church, Rhyl on 21st August, 1943.

Haul of Soldier Cyclists without lights

A batch of summonses on soldiers from Kinmel Park Camp were given at the Abergele Petty Sessions on 17th September, 1943. Fifteen shilling fines were imposed on **Lance Bombardier George H Leman**, **Gunner Yryriscow Charalambus**, **Sergeant Edward Naylor** and **Lance Corporal Thomas Newman**, **Gunner Archibald Kent**, and ten shilling fines for **Private Fred C Porter**, **Captain Howard Townsend**, **Gunner Joseph Harrison**, **Bombardier William Watson**, **Gunner Sidney Bocking**, **Gunner Ernest A Schofield**, and **Gunner William T Williams**.

Stolen Bike from the yard of his Former Employers
Edward L Jones

Gunner Edward L Jones aged 35, was sent to prison for one month with hard labour for stealing a bicycle from his former employer.

Committed two Rhyl Robbery's
(The Rhyl Journal 1st March, 1945)

George W Adams

Gunner George W Adams, gave himself up to Police after stealing a jacket, a pair of trousers, a scarf, shirt and tie, five sets of cuff links, a trilby hat, a tweed over coat and two pounds in cash. The property of Miss Barbra C Adams. Total value of the clothing was twenty four pounds. The items were stolen 24th – 26th February, 1945. Adams was discharged from the Army for being absent without leave by order of **Lt. Colonel H Greenwood, VC** *(Victoria Cross),* **DSO** *(Distinguished Service Order) and* **MC** *(Military Cross).*

Note: Lt. Colonel Harry Greenwood VC was one of the most decorated soldiers in the British Army. (VC, DSO and bar, MC, OBE and Mentioned in Despatches on several occasions) He has a book written about him, '**Valour Beyond all Praise**' by **Mr. Derek Hunt**. Adams was given a three-month jail sentence with hard labour by the civilian court.

Hit on the Head with Beer Bottle (The Rhyl Journal 29th March, 1945)

Harry Warwick

*Soldiers were sentenced for a savage attack on **Battery Quarter Master Sergeant Harry Warwick**, Kinmel Park Camp. The BQMS was assaulted with a beer bottle in Bodfor St, Rhyl by **Privates Goodie and Mellon**. They were sentenced to one month in jail with hard labour.*

Far too many cases of fraud on the Railway (The Rhyl Journal 16th August, 1945).

Ernst E Ramsey and John G Drudy

*Mr. **John Brookes** presiding at the Rhyl Petty Sessions warns against service personnel riding for free on our trains. Mr. Brookes fined **Gunner Ernst E Ramsey** of Kinmel Park Camp, one pound with ten shilling costs. He also fined **Gunner John G Drudy** of Sunnyvale Holiday Camp, ten shilling and five shilling costs.*

Slackness at Military Camp Alleged

Albert Edwards

A soldier, Gunner Albert Edwards of Head Quarters Battery, Search Light Wing, Royal Artillery, Kinmel Park Camp, did steal the following items on the 22nd July, 1945:- A joint of meat. On the 12th August, 1945 ,two cartons containing ninety-six tins of unsweetened milk, forty-eight tins of jam, with seven more tins on a small tray, fifteen pounds of pork, twenty eight pounds of sugar and another joint of meat, all the property of the War Department. All items were sold to Mr. Christopher E Osborne of Pensarn. Osborne was charged with receiving the goods knowing they were stolen.

Gunner Edwards was fined ten shilling for the two charges against him, Osborne however, was fined one pound on one count for receiving stolen goods, and two pounds on the second count.

Note: He got off lightly or what!?

Stole £1 off a Staff Sergeant

A thirteen year old boy pleaded guilty to the charge of stealing a one pound note from the coat pocket of Staff **Sergeant Reginald Kingdom,** of the Search Light Training Regiment, and a fifteen-year-old boy pleaded guilty of receiving five shillings of that money from the other boy, knowing it to have been stolen.

Staff Sergeant stated, "that during the afternoon of 12th October, he paid a visit to a woman friend residing at Mona Terrace, Rhyl, and whilst there, he left in his pocket, his wallet containing three pound notes, later he missed one". The matter was reported to the police, this lead to an investigation, which in turn lead to certain admissions by the two defendants. One of them said "they had spent some of the money on the slot machines", while the other said "he had hidden some of the money in the lavatory". Only seven shillings of the money was recovered. The bench decided to bind both boys over for two years in the sum of three pounds each, and ordered the payment of fifteen shilling costs.

Royal Artillery Memorial Service at Kinmel Park Camp

In keeping with the Royal Artillery Memorial Service, held at St. Pauls in London. On 4th December, 1945. 227 Royal Artillery Training

Regiment (Driver) will hold a Memorial Service at the Camp. Invitations were given to local families who lost relatives serving with the Royal Artillery during the Second World War.

Kinmel Camp Tragedy
John Jenner

The magistrates at the Abergle Police Courts were occupied for the whole of Saturday in connection with a recent Kinmel Camp tragedy, which resulted in the death of a young Manchester soldier and the wounding of another.

Private John Jenner (The Manchester Regiment) was charged with the wilful murder of Private John Victor Hawkins of Manchester Road, Heyward, Manchester, and a further charge of doing grievous bodily harm to Private Grindley by wounding with a bullet from a rifle.

Private Albert Hansen of Cardiff was charged with accessory before and after the fact. Both prisoners are mere youths, having just turned eighteen. Jenner being a native of London. Evidence was given that the prisoner Jenner was under detention in the Guard Room, and after being off fatigue work he returned to his cell. While the deceased soldier (Hawkins) Grindley and others were standing in front of the Battalion notice board, a shot was heard, and a bullet passed through Private Grindley and entered the left breast of Hawkins who died almost immediately. The Prosecution alleged that Jenner fired a rifle loaded with ball cartridge through a vent in his cell. When the guard went into his cell, they found Jenner lying on the ground trembling and excited. Company Sergeant Major Swarbrick said to Jenner "Do you know you have shot one of your own company boys". Jenner shook his head in response. Jenner had his rifle and equipment in his cell with him and a warm empty cartridge was found in his haversack. Swarbrick holding up the cartridge case asked Jenner "Did *you fire this"* Jenner answered in a low tone "Yes Sir, I did". In cross examination **Mr. Amos Jones** for the defence, said *"it was a pitiful state of affairs that no one seemed to know who put the man*

(Jenner) in his cell, or how he got his rifle equipment". **Lieutenant Roberts** said in his statement made to him by Jenner, that he, "Jenner was practicing loading and unloading his rifle". **Private Johnstone** said that while on fatigues that day with Jenner. Jenner told him that he was" going to shoot Sergeant Keeble". Jenner refused to proceed with his work and was taken to his cell by **Private Brown**. Jenner told witnesses "he had a rifle and live rounds, and these were given to him by **Private Hansen** and that he would have **Sergeant Keeble's** blood. Together with the Captain the Commanding officer and **Sergeant Wainwright**", he stated that he a" written their names on the wall of his cell". In cross examination the witness said "He thought Jenner was mad at the time". The Bench committed Jenner for trail on the charge of wilful murder. No Case Made Out. The charge against **Private Hansen** was then taken, the only witness called was **Private Johnstone** who gave evidence in the other case against Jenner. He stated that Hansen had told him "he had a bayonet, spanner and a jimi bar hidden under his pillow and he showed the witness (Johnstone) a belt full of ammunition" further stating "he had other cartridges in his putties". Asked what he intended doing with the cartridges, Hansen said "I shall make good use of them, to hold the guard up and get Jenner away or die in the attempt". After Hawkins was shot, he gave Jenner fourteen rounds of ammunition to kill Sergeant Keeble. The Bench said there was not enough evidence to go forward for trial and Hansen was discharged.

Points of Interest

During the Second World War and stationed at Kinmel Camp, was an Artillery Battery, held in support of the Search Light Unit, which was used to protect Liverpool from German Bomber attacks.

Note: Only one German bomb fell in the vicinity of Kinmel Camp during the Second World War. It was said to have blown the windows out of some buildings in the camp and at Bodelwyddan Castle which was used as a school for girls at that time.

Above: a Search-Light Unit crew (45)

There was no mention in the Rhyl Journal in regard to 'D Day', probably the most important event of the Second World War. The only mention to 'Victory in Europe Day' was that members of RAMTS were in attendance at the Old Comrades Club in Rhyl, reported in the Journal 23rd August, 1945.

"Victory" Mr. Churchill's historic announcement was given a write up on page five, plus a mention to the Rhyl Journals Staff taking their VE Day Holiday. Rhyl Journal dated 15th November, 1945 ran a short story about the Rhyl Council Chairman 'Remembers'.

The first mention in five years of the laying of a wreath at the Rhyl Cenotaph. Also a spate of weddings were reported in the Rhyl Journal, of soldiers marrying local girls, especially from Kinmel Park Camp. One wedding in particular stood out.

Marriage

Lance Bombardier J. S Conavan, Royal Artillery, Kinmel Park Camp to Miss Joyce Dean at St. Margaret's Church, Bodelwyddan reported in the Rhyl Journal 5th July, 1945.

Private 59523 Fletcher.

Fletcher of the 53rd Young Soldier Battalion (The Liverpool

Regiment) D Company was posted to camp 17, at Kinmel Camp, the 53rd where formerly known as the 72nd Young Soldiers Battalion, and before that they were known as the 21st Battalion of the Lancashire Fusiliers.

Rhyl Indoor Swimming Baths

During WW2, the swimming baths on Sussex Street, Rhyl was seconded to Kinmel Camp and used as a storage facility for the duration of the war.

Westcliffe Garage, Rhyl

As well as the swimming pool in Rhyl being requisitioned by the Army at Kinmel Camp for the storage of vehicles and equipment, so was Westcliffe Garage on Wellington Street, Rhyl.

War Poems written by locals published in the Rhyl Journal

"A Cup of Tea"

*Other armies have their coffee their lager and wine
I don't say nowt against them – they are fine!
But the British Tommie's fancy wherever he may be, is the
stuff that he gets at home – a grand old cup of tea.
Maybe greasy, thick as treacle, wet and warm or simply rank.
But always very welcome in the trench or tank.*

He has fought all around the world to keep our people free and is doing it again, on many, many cups of Rosie Lea. **(Rhyl Journal 10th March 1944).**

"A Score to Settle"

*He's got something of the Bull Dog
He's as strong as any Ox and he's used to freez-
ing nights and in the blazing sun.
He can give it – he can take it.*

For he has learned to take hard knocks.
He's got a score to settle with the Hun
Since the day he was sworn in, as a very raw recruit.
He has sworn to make the Jerries run.
So pay homage to the soldier, and let's give him a salute.
For we have all a score to settle with the Hun.

(Rhyl Journal dated 3ʳᵈ February, 1944).

These are just two of many poems written by locals and published in the Rhyl Journal.

Army Cadet Force

Towards the end of the Second World War, there are mentions to The Army Cadets using Kinmel Park Camp. One event, was the 2nd Battalion the Royal Welsh Fusiliers, who took up residence in the first week of August 1944 for their annual camp.

Note: The Welsh Army Cadet Force use the camp to this day.

Bates/Millard Marriage

Miss Lillian Bates worked for the **NAAFI (Navy, Army, Air Force, Institute)** during the Second World War at Kinmel Camp, and where Lilly met her future husband **Roger Millard,** a serving soldier.

The Milk Problem

During the 1930's, questions were asked as to why the camp was being supplied foreign milk and as to how much milk was being supplied by local farmers. It was stated that the supply of milk was up to each individual Commanding Officers of the Territorial Units, using the camp facility for the training of their men. The supply of milk was of great importance to the local farmers, as there was a glut of milk at that time. It only made sense to use this means of supply to the camp. I wonder how this was resolved, common sense I would like to think.

Married Quarters at Kinmel

The following were built for the Permanent Staff for the quartering of their families. 1-24 Artillery Drive, 1-4 and 7-10 St. Barbaras Avenue, 1-56 Coronation Close, 1-8 Hillcrest Court.

CHAPTER 10

POST WAR KINMEL -
THE COLDEST OF WINTERS -1947

After completing his initial training at Ballykinler in Northern Ireland, Driver Sidney Knight was sent to Kinmel Camp, it was early in the winter of 1947. That winter was one of the worst in recorded history. The Military Hospital in Chester (The Deva) was running short of fuel. Knight was ordered to pick up two German POW's and proceed to a coal mine near to Prestatyn, they were to pick up supplies and then deliver them to Chester. The trip almost took them three days to complete, due to the deep snow drifts they encounted on their trip.

The names of soldiers who also trained at Kinmel

James Alfred Hooper during 1944, **Gunner's George Johnson** and **Fred Booth** were at Kinmel for their Basic Training, late 1947 to early 1948.

Harold Maidstone 1947 – 1960 as a soldier and a civilian Driving Instructor.

In the Fifties at Kinmel Park
In the fifties the camp became the home to the Boys Battery, Royal Artillery.

The Globe Cinema

A new management took over the Goble **Mr. Vernon Hobbs** with his wife during the 1960's.

Above: Training Staff (Section 1 – 81st Training Battery, Royal Artillery in August 1956 (46)

21 Gun Salute in Colwyn Bay

A 21 gun salute was carried out by members of Kinmel Camp (Royal Artillery) in Colwyn Bay on promenade by kind permission of the Commanding Officer.

Above: a Battery of 3.7 Heavy Anti-Aircraft Guns, the type that were used in Colwyn Bay (47)

Cup Winners (NWCFA)

In the football season of 1948-49 the Training Regiment Artillery (**31 and 38 Regiments**) won the North Wales Junior Cup, their first and only time.

Search Light Tattoo

The Commanding Officer of Kinmel Camp with the co-operation of W. R Watkins of the North Wales Magic Circle held a Search Light Tattoo in 1948 on the Camp, it was such a success that it was repeated in 1949.

Boys to Man's Service (The Trumpeter)

Gunner Dave Flett left the Boys Regiment at Kinmel Camp in the April, 1953. However, due to his age he was only 17 years and 6 months he was posted immediately back to Kinmel, along with some others of the same age. He was given a course as a Despatch Rider, on its completion he was posted to 40 Field Regiment Royal Artillery (The Lowland Gunners).

Gunner A.I Morrison Royal Artillery

Gunner 23114203 Morrison completed his basic Training at the 31st Training Regiment Kinmel Camp in North Wales. After his basic training was completed he was given a driving course. On completion he was posted to 77 HAA Regiment in Delmenhorst, British Army on the Rhine.

Bombardier 23211622 Eric Brown Royal Artillery

Bombardier Brown was called forward for his National Service having his medical in Croydon, he was passed as A1 fit. However, instead of doing National Service he decided to sign up as a Regular Soldier on a 22 year engagement, which was as known as a lifer. He did this to ensure a posting abroad and collect overseas allowance (more money in his pocket). I wanted to join the Royal Artillery and by signing as a Regular I got my wish. My first posting was to Kinmel Camp in North Wales, my first day at Kinmel was the 13th July, 1954.

Gunner Neville Shucksmith 40 Field Regiment RA 1957/58.

Gunner Joseph Blades. (57/10)

Gunner John Dougherty (Feb /Jun 57)

Gunner Geoff Brown and **Gunner B. A Jones.** (59/6)

Gunner George Peacock 21 Medium Regiment RA (60/61)

The first thing we did on the morning of our first day was physical training in PT vest and shorts. Basic training is exactly as it sounds 'Basic'. Intakes rotated through in three monthly cycles. It consisted of hundreds of teenagers from all walks of life doing their Basic. The main rule was if anyone in authority told you to do something no matter how dumb it sounded, you did it without question. Once a week there was a Barrack Inspection by the intake Officer and Sergeant. We only had one iron between twenty of us, sometimes you would be waiting until the early hours to get your turn, in order to conform to your layout of your uniform. There were times when a chaps kit was not up to snuff, only to be ordered by the officer to throw their kit out of the window, followed by the defaulter going outside to march all over his kit. (Being in Wales it was more often than not, wet). This was followed by get your kit together and I will re-inspect it first thing in the morning. The defaulter would be up all night putting it right. I must admit I enjoyed basic training, especially drill (marching) and small arms drill. At the end of my initial training I was selected to join the Con Troop (Continuation Troop) here we were given training on the 3.7 Heavy Anti-Aircraft Guns. We had a Royal Marine Drill Sergeant, he instructed us on various marching skills and formations (Ceremonial Drill) and I enjoyed every minute of it. Eventually after 162 days my training at Kinmel Camp came to an end and I was posted to Hong Kong on the 22nd December 1954.

Above: Flash of the Apprentices Army Junior Tradesmen's Regiment (48)

Beaters

5th January 1965 saw fifty men detailed off (volunteered) to be Beaters for the day, paid ten shillings each in extra duty pay the men were members of the 38th Regiment RA. Questions were asked about the use of soldiers for this external pass time. It was said the Commanding Officers can use their men as they see fit even though the event was a civilian event. I guess nothing changes!

Gunner 23187889 Clayton G

Above: A Christmas card by Gnr G Clayton RA (49)

George Layton's story of his time at Kinmel Camp during the 1950's. A reluctant conscript, stated he made friends for life. Only realising what a rich experience it was to be young and mostly skint, but free and happy and in great company. George made a good friend whilst at Kinmel **Gnr Joe Sweeney**, one story Joe told George was that of a mock Irish Republican Army raid on the camp, staged by 5 young subalterns in 1954. In the August of 1955 the IRA raided Aborfield Barracks, Berkshire. The seed was sown so to speak, as the young subalterns though it would be a good prank to stage a mock raid on Kinmel, trying to gain access to the main Guard Room and then the Armoury. Their actions were foiled, local Police Stations were put on alert. A few days after the incident the subalterns decided to own up to their prank. An enquiry was set up in Shrewsbury, with all involved being posted out of the unit. They were very lucky young men indeed. George had never met an aristocrat in his life until he met **Lt. Colonel Lord Langford** the Commanding Officer of the 31st Regiment Royal Artillery, an ebullient, blimpish, over bearing, impressive larger than life officer, and a force to be reckoned with. A man of habit who took a half of bitter on most days when in the Mess. Not once did he make eye contact with the young Barman Clayton, nonetheless he was a likeable man. His turnout at Mess functions was immaculate, together with a golden decoration which hung around his neck and a chest full of medals. At the end of the mess dinner many traditions were carried out including that of the young officers making a canon and by chopping match heads off and loading then into the bottom of an aluminium cigar tube, adding a smaller cigar tube to the top, positioning the newly made weapon which was supported by two dinner forks, they were then heated at the base by using matches for a few seconds, which was followed by an small explosion and a cloud of smoke, the head of the projectile arced across the table, if by chance it hit anywhere near it's intended target a huge roar would erupt from fellow officers. Lord Langford was a hero in his own right, during the fall of Singapore he with some other officers organised an escape, sailing 1500 miles across the Bay of Bengal to Ceylon. A book written by Ian Sinclair (In the late 60's early 70's) tells of the heroic efforts made by these men. Lord Langford passed away on 12th November, 2017 at the age of 105. After initial training George took up a position in the Officers Mess. **Lt. Col W Lyon** the Commanding Officer of 38 Training Regiment, was completely the opposite of Lord Langford. At 6' 6" and ever the total gentleman, a fine sportsman who played cricket for the Royal Artillery. A creature of habit who frequented the Officers Mess every evening drinking his usual tipple of a double gin with a vermouth mixer. A great one for storytelling, stories about his time in India and his service during the Second World War amongst his fellow officers.

Above: The officers Mess bar staff. Gnr Clayton bottom right (50)

Another individual George remembers from his time in recruit training was **Sergeant David Cutliffe** who certainly looked after his charges. However, he did not like being posted to Kinmel Camp and constantly applied for posting abroad. Eventually he was posted to Cyprus. The island was at the time in the throes of an emergency, with a civil war between Greeks and Turks. Sgt Cutliffe and his family were out shopping in Nicosia on the city's Main Mile when Mrs Cutliffe was shot and killed, the story made all the papers at that time. Young Clayton's watering hole during his 2 years at Kinmel was a local public house the Ty Fry, over the decades thousands of servicemen and women have frequented the establishment. Many a song was sang and a light swung over the years and many going back to barracks penniless but happy. George remembers the private school in the grounds of Bodelwyddan Castle for the daughters of the wealthy. School holiday time was an eye opener with fleets of limousines arriving to take the pampered young ladies home. In spite of its proximity to the Camp the young ladies were never exposed to the ruffians next door. However, there was the odd compliant of young soldiers scaling the walls to get a look at the girls. Now and again the staff of the Lowther School were guests of the officer's mess, the contact being most appropriate as they were between the same social classes.

CHAPTER 11

THE SIXTIES AT KINMEL PARK CAMP

The Regular Army took over Kinmel in the 1960's, and became the home of the Junior Tradesmen's Regiment. Young Boys were accepted from the age of fifteen and three months. They were given extensive military training, before moving onto various Royal Artillery Regiments. At the age of seventeen and six months. The first intake was January of 1962, and the final intake was in July 1974, when it officially closed. It must be noted that those young boys believed they had entered a special Brotherhood, that for them, has lasted down the years. One boy commented that:

"The Junior Tradesman's Regiment experience was a special time for them all, it became their home and the only family they had never known".

The following are extracts from a friends ramblings, **Mr. Mike Bartie** an 'old fart' from 1964's initial training at Kinmel Park Camp:

"How the hell do you dust water Corporal" a question given to a Junior None Commissioned Officer, by a raw recruit during a room inspection.

Above: The Sign, that greeted young men to Kinmel Camp (51)

On the 8ᵗʰ January 1964, the young Master Bartie (also known as,

*Pheat) caught the bus to Oldham town centre, and then caught a train to Manchester Exchange Station. He then walked the short distance to Piccadilly and found a seat on the train to Rhyl, North Wales. The train was full of young lads all going to the same place. The train stopped at every station in those days. During the journey, the lads got to know each other with things getting pretty rowdy and plenty of laughter. Having spoken with the other lads, Bartie found out that nearly everyone on board was bound for Rhyl. They were all about to start the first day of their lives. On arrival at Rhyl Station, he wondered how he was to find Kinmel Park Camp. There was no problem, as there was a rather large reception committee. After much shouting everyone was lined up at the tables provided, where names were taken and crossed off the arrivals list. Eventually, every-one was loaded onto army trucks and driven to the camp. Kinmel Park Camp was miles from anywhere, near a small village which nobody could pronounce. (Bodelwyddan). Also known to young Bartie as 'Boddly-Widdly' to this day. Dumped outside of Cambrian Company Lines, Junior NCOs were buzzing around telling us who was in which Platoon, and our names were on the front door to the allotted billet. Cambrian Company was where new recruits did their basic training, before moving onto trade or continuation training. No sooner had we put our suit cases down, we were marched off to the bedding store to collect bedding. We were also given more stuff than we could possibly carry. The storemen shouting what items they were giving us and asking for signatures before sending us back to our billet to make our beds. 'Who knew how to make a bed?' It was not long before a Sergeant came into the billet and introduced himself, "I am **Sergeant Leckie** of the Welsh Regiment and I am your Platoon Sergeant". He gave us a short briefing on what we were to expect over the next few days, and how the system worked. We were taken to the camp cinema and were given various presentations from the Camp Commanding Officer **Lt. Colonel Whalen**, of the Duke of Edin-burgh's Royal Regiment and **Regimental Sergeant Major Morgan**, Royal Army Service Corps. Our Company Commander was **Major Williams** and our **Company Sergeant Major Rogers** Grenadier Guards. This was followed by a tour of the camp lines. Then a short* *trip to the cook house, we would get to know this place well. Amazingly, the first night on camp was ours, so we were told. We were told to get to know each other. Lights out was 2230 hours, and we fell into our pits/beds after a long whirlwind of a day. The next day was another whirlwind of administration, medicals (cough, jabs, etc) more kit issues. Our JNCOs moving us about as a massed rabble, attempting to get us to march as a body of men, hard work initially. Off for haircuts we went. Short back and sides being the only hair cut on offer or so we* thought, *none of that, the cut was to the wood. Bartie had his hair cut done before leaving Oldham. Sgt Leckie ripped Bartie up on that one, stating "You were robbed son, they saw you coming". No body laughed at any one once they left the chair, as each one of us looked the same, a bloody borstal boy. We took a long time sorting out our uniforms, ironing, what is ironing? Bulling boots, now there is something that will never be forgotten once learned. Blanco your webbing, polish your brasses to a high shine, even putting studs into your boots and in the correct pattern, shaping you leather boot laces, shrink and shape your beret it went on and on, followed by bed blocks and locker lay outs. Bartie was given a regimental number ending with 666 the devils number, more by accident than by anything as he and another recruit were given the same regimental number, on the toss of a coin Bartie was 23990666. The only good thing about his number was it was easy to remember.*

Above Left: The Bed Block, laid out every day by all recruits during their initial training (52)

Above Right: Barrack ready for inspection (53)

Our first parade with uniform on, was an absolute stinker, well at least the mothballed uniforms we wore stunk. Once the usual bollocking for being a shower of shite was given to us all, it was drill, drill followed by even more drill. We are in the bloody army now, that is for sure. After lunch, we were shown how to lay our kit on our beds and in our lockers. Each man given a diagram of the layout expected. One thing puzzled us, we'd been given brown plimsolls and being told to polish them black. Why not issue black ones in the first place?. I guess nothing is simple in the army. The worst bit of kit issued to us was the physical training kit and especially the shorts, they were always too big and baggy for the individual, having to press creases into them, knowing that once you had worn them for training, they would need to be washed and ironed all over again. Something no one saw, was the issued underpants, nick-named draws 'Dracula' or 'Drakes'. Uniform was known as 'Itchy and Scratchy', a woollen jacket and trousers, known as Battle Dress and of course a khaki flannel shirt to complete the misery especially in the summer. What with the heat! Sweat rashes were the order of the day.

Above: Junior Trooper Jenkins, 1st The Queens Dragoon Guards (54)

Wearing his battle dress uniform. (Dave Jenkins sadly passed away in May, 2015 whilst on holiday in Malta aged 64)

**Above: Trooper Stephen Carter (QDG) the gym
in the back ground (55)**

Bored! Let's run the Gauntlet

Running the gauntlet was were all the lads in your room lined up either side of the beds, and one brave or on may occasion a not so brave individual, would attempt to run from one end of the room to the other. As soon as the individual was within range, everyone battered him stupid. Character building or what!

The Pillow Fight

As the name suggests, a free-for-all, last man standing was the winner, batter one and all. The night before the Commanding Officers inspection all hell broke out. A bar room brawl had nothing on what occurred this night in our billet. Kit lays outs went for a ball of chalk, lads from adjoining rooms ran in to our room and joined in the free for all. Ten minutes of hell only ended when the duty Sergeant entered the room. **Sergeant McCauley** shouting his head off in an attempt to get our attention, this he eventually did, **Speedy Freedman** was the last man to come to heel, there were duck feathers everywhere. We took both barrels, a tirade of abuse, with his final comment being," gentlemen luckily for you that there is a Commanding Officers inspection in the morning, now get this place sorted". Now **Freedman** was detailed to pick up every feather with a fork, and place them back into his pillow case, both inside and outside of the barrack room.

Promotion to Room Senior – The Curse of being a Switched on Cookie

This happened to many a young man who was considered that much further advanced than his peers. The chosen individual, was the butt on which all discrepancies were hurled by the Company Sergeant and Corporals, commonly known amongst the boys as the poison chalice.

The Regimental Bath (The punishment given to a 'Grunge')

The Reggie bath usually given to the soldier who did not take care of his personal hygiene. Often the individual would be taken screaming from his pit/bed to the washrooms, were he would be subject to a bath given by his peers, ice cold water, vim or washing powder poured all over the chap, then scrubbed with all types of bushes from head to toe. This treatment in the main worked, but there were the odd one or two who would get a second helping, at some time during their basic training. Most, if not all, those given the Reggie bath would come back into their billet and say there were sorry to his peers. Normally the improvement of the individual's appearance would change drastically for the good of the individual, and believe it or not, the good of all his peers in his billet.

The Church Parade

This was compulsory on Sunday morning, there was no way of dodging it. The roll was called, and then the young soldiers were marched to church.

Above: inside one of the churches at Kinmel Camp (56)

The Pay Parade

Soldiers got their wages on pay parades, the Pay Master (an officer) would be sat behind a table usually in the corridor. Stood behind him would be two volunteer witnesses, Their job would be to check the amount the Pay Master calls out to each soldiers receiving his pay. They ensure that he counts out the correct amount before handing it the individual. Young soldiers had to be coached on how this parade went, days before the pay parade. Most young men would be shaking in their boots by this process, after having your name called giving the reply of "Sir" at the top of their voice and marching smartly into position in front of the desk, followed by the smartest salute one could give. Number, Rank and Name. The Pay Master would then tell the individual what he was to receive. The soldier would then sign his personal pay book, stating "pay and pay book correct, Sir". Followed by one pace step backwards, a salute, neat about turn and smartly march away. The hope of every man jack was to get this right, many had to do it twice and some thrice. It was the most nerve racking parade you ever had to do.

Out of Bounds

There were out of bounds area within the camp. Basically it was everywhere above the level of the cookhouse. Should you be caught in an OOB area, the price would be death by a million cuts or so it felt, to the miscreant who ventured there.

The Cookhouse

Those who entered the cookhouse for the first time found it quite daunting. Soldiers were given a green plastic mug, so mug in hand one entered. Oh! I forgot to say that you had to march smartly to the cookhouse with mug firmly behind your back. The first thing you noticed was the bigger boys who were in the advanced training companies. They took precedence, simply by the fact that they had been at the establishment longer than you, speak up and you would get a clip around the ear, just for starters. Eventually you found your depth, sitting with all the new guys, until such time as a new intake arrived and then you moved up the pecking order.

Weapons Training

At Kinmel, we had a small arms instructor, **Sergeant Storm** of the Light Infantry. He was carved out of shear granite! I assure you. After teaching dry drills in slow, slow time. He would then give us a full speed demonstration, while calling out all the moves. He completely intimidated us all by how good he was. After much failure on weapon , things fell into place and we passed although by the skin of our teeth.

Physical Training

Prior to any session in the gym you had a full inspection, if your plimsolls were still brown, the bollocking of your life befell your ears. If your shorts were creased another bollocking came your way, same with your PT vest. The instructors would then take you for a wee beasting, all prior to the gym session. Although the sessions were hard at first, over time they became quite enjoyable. After six weeks you would do a fitness test. This would show the Physical Training Instructors how much you had progressed physically. Once the basic level had been achieved, games would be played, boxing, five-a-side football and killer ball. Most if not all sessions were over seen by **Company Sergeant Major Senior Master Instructor Cai**n, of the APTC and a Civvy named **Mr. White** who was over 50 and super fit and a couple of **Corporals Powell** RASC and **Oakley** RA. Oakley was always growling at us, he was not a happy chappie.

Drill

This was a never ending chore which had to be instilled into us. We lived on the drill square during the initial six weeks. For those who did their training at Kinmel Camp gloves were not worn in the winter months, understandable when it came to rifle drill. The RSM or the CSM would take the drill sessions; we were scared witless by them. **WO1 Regimental Sergeant Major Morgan** was a scary man. You would walk hundreds of yards off your route, rather than march past his office window. No one got past his window without a bollocking for something or other. He looked like a tailors dummy in a shop window, nothing was out of place. His boots were like glass and his haircut, the sides where shaved up to his hat band, thus making his head shine. (His hair was shorter than ours, now that says something).

'O Grady Says'

The RSM would play a game with us new boys called 'O Grady Says. The RSM would give words of command preceded with the words 'O Grady Say'; you dare not move if these words were not spoken, if you moved without those words of caution you were out, marched to the side of the square. The game was last man standing. The early days of drill was geared to our pass off parade (normally five or six weeks). You had to be able to march up to an officer and halt, salute and address him, reply to any response, salute, about turn and march smartly away. Quite nerve racking for any new recruit. The half term pass off parade, which was for new recruits, a short parade which allowed family and friends to see how well you were adapting to army life. Once you accomplished this event, it was two weeks leave. When you returned, you moved up to trade training and were allowed down town, albeit in uniform. So ends the story of young Bartie and his basic training. There were thousands of young men who went through basic training at Kinmel Camp, and in the army in general almost all mirroring the above experiences. Those were the days hey!

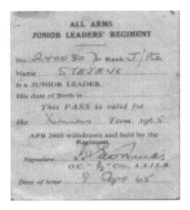

Above: The Leave Pass, without one of these a young soldier could not leave camp (57)

Above: Some Members of the Permanent Staff Kinmel Park Camp during its time as the All Arms Junior Training Regiment (58)

The Junior Leaders Training Regiment was formed in 1962 it was disbanded in 1974.

Above: The Regimental Plaque (59)

Above: Young soldiers from 1971 posing during a field craft exercise (60)

A few names of boys who were trained at Kinmel Camp during the 1960's, are **Mr. Jack Williams**, **Mr. Mike Vowels** and **Mr. Frank Gibbons, George Peacock, Mike Potts, Bob Jeary and John Sleight** representing thousands of young men who passed through the gate.

Clwyd County Council makes their decision on the future of Kinmel Park Camp

Kinmel Park Camp is declared surplus to the Ministry of Defence requirements with effect from 20th November, 1973. At the time, two hundred and ninety nine acres. This includes ninety eight acres of hutted accommodation, garages, workshops and parade grounds, plus thirty two acres laid out for Driver Training and sixteen acres of residential properties (which included one hundred married quarters). Fifty nine acres of agricultural land (the general training area) and twenty three acres of recreational land to the North of the A55 are to be sold.

Above: is a diagram map of Kinmel Park Camp, it once was the biggest training facility in Wales (61)

Note: this was the second time in its lifetime in which part of the camp would be sold off.

Territorial Units at Kinmel Park
3rd Battalion the Royal Welsh Fusilier's. The local Territorial Unit and the Cadet Forces used the camps facilities until the middle of the 90's. The newly formed **Royal Welsh Regiment** are frequent users of the camp.

Today, in 2019 there is a small part of the camp and its training area left. This is used mainly by the Cadet Forces. The rest the camp area was sold off to the private sector, and there are various factories and units on the former camp. However, the foot print of Kinmel Park Camp is there for all to see, you can still see the training trenches, these can be seen from the air. Plans are afoot to establish the trench system, as part of the project named under the Twentieth Century Military Project ,together with the Clwyd-Powys Archaeological trust.

Above: A small part of the training trenches, which can be seen in the training area at Bodelwyddan Castle (62)

A Great War Trench Rebuilt

It would be amiss of me not to include the story about a new trench system at Bodelwyddan Castle. The trench system was built in memory of all those young men who passed through Kinmel Park Camp during the Great War. There is an area of the trench dedicated to the Canadian Riot at the camp, and the lives of local men. Also included into the trench system, is a Regimental Aid Post and Officer's Dugout. All this was built by a dedicated trench team of historians, researchers and volunteers. Well worth a visit by historians of The Great War.

National Police Air Service at Kinmel Park Camp Helicopter Flight.

The camp was used for quite some time in the nineties (94-99) by North Wales Police as a base for their Helicopter.

Above: Police Helicopter's based at Kinmel Camp (G-NWPI) (63)

Below: The Euro Copter EC-135 (G-NWPS) (64)

There is not much to report about the time it was based at Kinmel Camp, but one funny story was told, that one night a young man from the Wrexham area, Mr. Gareth Ieuan Roberts aged 30, did brake into the the camp and inparticlar the heli pad. He managed to get into the helicopoter; he was caught at the controls. It is believed he had learnt how to do this from his laptop. He was arrested and charged by North Wales Police for attempting to steal a Eurocopter EC-135 worth 2 million pounds. I think the camp secuirty must have been reviewed after this incident. Amazingly, Roberts did not receive a custodial sentence.

The Military Training Awareness Course – Kinmel Camp

Above: Instructors and Students of one of the many course held at Kinmel Camp (65)

North Wales Training - Youth Engagement Team

A leading supplier of vocational training for N. Wales it was established in 1983. It provides youth, a head start in finding the right job for them, offering military themed programs which include (1) The School Engagement, this is for 11-16-year olds, both military and non-military. (2) Post 16 Traineeships, these are for 16-18 year olds, both military and civilian related. (3) Corporate Program, covers things such as first aid team building etc. Although they run military courses in the main, they are not trying to turn each individual who gets involved into these programs as soldiers, rather than teaching them the values of being responsible young persons, who are able to work as individuals or as part of a team. It is great to see that Kinmel Camp is being used for this purpose. Following in the footsteps of oh! so many young men.

Private Sam Owen

Sam Owen took part in the Military Training Course after leaving school. He says that the course was "brilliant" and a must for young adults with an eye to joining the Armed Forces. Sam joined the army for his initial training at Harrogate and has not looked back.

The Primary Resources used in this book

Mr. Philip G. Hindley of Old Colwyn – The Kinmel Camp Railway – some stories have been included.

Colonel Howard J. Coombs - Canadian Armed Forces – The Apathetic and Defiant some excerpts have been included.

Mr. Julian Putkowski – The Kinmel Park Riots 1919 – some resorces have been included.

The Rhyl Journal 1914-1918 and 1939 1945 – some extracts have been included.

The Rhyl Advertiser 1914-1918 – some extracts have been included.

The North Wales Advertiser – some extracts have been included.

Mr. Steven John – The Carmarthen Pals – some extracts have been included.

Mr. Mike Bartie - My time at the Army Apprentice's Junior Training Regiment – some extracts have been included.

Mr. Tony Derbyshire a local historian (**Colwyn Bay)** Canadian posts cards have been included.

The Flintshire Archives – some extracts and pictures have been included.

Mr. Robert Griffiths – The Story of Kinmel Park Military Training Camp 1914-1918 – some resources have been included.

Mr. Robert Griffiths- Riots, Death and Baseball, The Canadians at Kinmel Park 1918-19 – some resources have been included.

Mr. Gareth Jones – information provided on his Great Uncle Lcpl Ivor Morgan SWB.

The Abergele Visitor – some extracts have been included.

The Liverpool Daily Post – some extracts have been included.

London Gazette – some extracts have been included.

The Glamorgan Gazette – some extracts have been included.

The North Wales Chronicle and Advertiser for the Principality – some extracts have been included.

The Clwyd-Powys-Archaeological Trust – some photographs have been included.

Hawarden Public Library for their assistance.

Alan Greveson's WW1 Forum – some extracts have been included.

www.rhonddaremembers.com – some extracts form Sergeant Thomas Price's diary (13th Battalion Welsh Regiment). Have been included.

Some extracts of the Dairy **of George John Culpitt** curtesy of his son **Mr. Peter Culpitt.**

Some Extracts from **Trafaion Gymdeith Hanes-y- Bedyddwyr 2001**.

 Some extracts from the **"Trumpeter" No17 of January 2015.**

Some extracts from **"A False Sense of Security" by Mr. Simon James Theobald.**

Some extracts from **the Kings Own Royal Regiment.**

Some extracts from **Richard Thomas's memories of his Great Grandfather Francis Thomas Royal Welsh Fusiliers.**

Some extracts from **Mr. Neil Evans,** a letter written to me telling me of his relation **Sgt Leonard (John) Nuttall the Welsh Regiment.**

Mr. George Clayton (RA) letters and pictures.

The Canadian War Museum at 1, Vimy Place, Ottawa, Canada

Mrs Sue Pugh, of Whitcourst, Alberta for the article out her relation who served during The Great War.

My **most sincere apologies** to anyone or organisation who I may have mistakenly omitted from the list above. I trust I have done all the resources used in the writing of this book proud, and all their names are recorded within.

Utmost thanks to **Major Floyd Low CD** for his much-appreciated help from Ottawa, Canada and his comments on the first draft version of this book, also to **Colonel Howard Coombs CD** for his comments of the second draft reading.

A big thank you to my wife **Jacqueline Johnson (Jaci)** for reading and producing the final draft of this book. Without your help, it may have never been finished.

A very special thank you to **Mr. Tom Burke** for the amazing book cover design. Lastly, the greatest appreciation of thanks goes to my wife **Jaci** for all her support and patience over the last six years. There must have been times that she thought she was single and our living room a very was lonely place.

Chapter 12

In memory of those servicemen and women who died whilst serving at Kinmel Park Camp during the First World War

'Lest We Forget'

Private Armstrong Thomas, of the Welsh Regiment, accidentally drowned on the 3rd July, 1915. Aged 17.

Private Edward Akers, aged 26, took his own life by jumping off the Foryd Bridge, Rhyl. He left a wife and two young children.

Corporal John T Breakingbury, of the 12th Battalion the Welsh Regiment, dropped dead on the 15th December, 1915. Whilst giving directions for a bugle call, the cause of his death was given as natural causes.

Private David A Evans, aged 28, of the 3rd Training Battalion Welsh Regiment. Died of pneumonia on the 14th February, 1917. At the camp hospital.

Private John Jones, aged 28, of the 20th Battalion Welsh Regiment Training Reserve Battalion, Kinmel Park Camp. He died on the 27th February, 1917. Cause of his death was tuberculosis.

Specialist Enlistment Soldier Humphrey Davies RTS/3665 aged 38, enlisted into the 2nd Brigade Army Service Corps – 2nd Remount Section. A unit that dealt with horses. He was sent to France with the British Expeditionary Force serving with 2nd Remount Army Service Corps, as a shoeing smith/farrier for the period 29th October, 1914 to 16th September, 1916. While in France, Davis became quite ill and was returned to the UK eventually ending up in Kinmel Park Camp, where he was to convalesce. However, his health deteriorated and was diagnosed as having anaemia. On the 13th March, 1917. He passed away in the camp hospital. His post mortem result gave cause of death as cancer of the stomach.

Private Richard P Thompson, of the 12th Battalion Welsh Regiment, died from head injuries caused by a fall from a buckboard. Thompson died on the 3rd February, 1916.

Acting Corporal Robert L , aged 43, of the 2nd Battalion Welsh Regiment, and **Private Francis Thomas** aged 37, of the same Regiment, were walking back towards Kinmel Park Camp at 2200 hours (On the St. Asaph Road near to Nant Ddu) when they were hit by a bus and killed.

Private Robert Owen, of the 20th (Reserve) Battalion the Royal Welsh Fusiliers, died on the 1st April, 1916 aged 18. At Bangor Military Hospital.

Private William J Jones 13th Battalion of the South Wales Borders aged 32, having taken his own life on 10th April, 1916. He is buried at Abergele Cemetery, North. Wales.

Private Hughie Edwards of the 14th Battalion South Wales Borders, died on 5th April,1916. Edwards died at Bangor Military Hospital after a short illness (pneumonia). This young soldier's death was questioned in an exchange between Sir H. Roberts and Mr. Tennant (the Under Secretary for War) in the House of Commons.

Corporal Evan Daniels of the 13th Battalion South Wales Borderers, aged 53, was hit and killed by a motor vehicle on his way back towards Kinmel Camp from Rhyl.

Private Thomas Walsh of the 13th Battalion South Wales Borderers, died at Bangor Military Hospital from Spotted Fever, otherwise known as cerebrospinal meningitis. It was noted that other soldiers from Kinmel Camp died of this disease whilst in training at the Camp. On May 6th, 1916. It was reported in the North Wales Times that the Camp was said by some observers *"Not to be good enough for German Prisoners Of War, but alright from an official point of view for the British Tommy"*.

Private Albert Matthews aged 19 , of the 2nd Battalion Royal Fusiliers, was taken ill, and within an hour, he was taken to Bangor Military Hospital and died.

Note: I wrote a more in depth short story earlier in this book about Private Matthews.

Lance Sergeant James J Willoughby and **Private Albert Cleaver**, aged 30, both 20th Battalion the Welsh Regiment, were accidently killed whilst undergoing training on the grenade range.

Lance Sergeant Nuttall, of the 12th Reserve Battalion Royal Welsh Fusiliers, took his own life (by hanging in Bryn Elwy Wood near St Asaph) on the 25th June, 1916. Nuttall was sent to France in 1915, and took part in the Battle of Loos. He committed suicide while temporarily insane.

Above: Lance Sergeant Nuttall (66)

Private John Carney, aged 40, of the 12th Battalion the Royal Welsh Fusiliers, died of heart failure whilst in training at Kinmel

Park Camp on the 14th July, 1916.

Private Arthur W Charles, aged 19, died on the 6th August, 1916. He was a member of the 20th Battalion the Welsh Regiment (also known as the 3rd Rhondda Reserve Battalion. He was taken ill and sent initially to the Camp Hospital; he was then transferred to Bangor Military Hospital where he passed away.

Second Lieutenant John E Mathias, aged 37, of the 5th Battalion the Welsh Regiment, was found drowned 11th October, 1916, in a pond just 100 yards from his billet.

Private Ernest Clark, formerly of the South Wales Borderers, was hit and killed by a motor vehicle whilst walking along the Abergele to Bodelwyddan Road, on 23rd December, 1916. He was conveyed to Kinmel Camp where he died of his injuries.

Lieutenant William Reece, of the 15th Battalion Welsh Regiment attached to the 3rd Welsh Regiment. He passed away in his bed on the 2nd February, 1917. Lieutenant Reece had been at Kinmel Park Camp for just 56 hours before his passing. He died of natural causes. (There is a more in-depth article on William within this book)

Private William H Gay, aged 45, of the 3rd Garrison Battalion (Labour Battalion) Royal Welsh Fusiliers, dropped dead whilst on a platoon march to Abergele Railway Station. The last words spoken by Gay were *"I am done"*. Cause of death heart failure.

Driver Alfred J Ellis, of the Royal Army Service Corps 49th company, was killed in a road traffic accident on the 14th February, 1917. He was thrown from his horse and float, and then ran over by a bus (the Silver Motor Company) ,whilst on a duty trip to Abergele. Ellis was taken to Kinmel Park Hospital; he was pronounced dead on arrival.

Private William Luke, of the Army Service Corps attached to 64th Training Reserve Battalion, aged 19, died on the 13th March,1917. Cause of death was a haemorrhage and burst blood vessel.

Second Lieutenant Arthur W Martin, aged 31, serving with the 61st Training Reserve Battalion the Welsh Regiment, died of the result of an accident at the grenade range at Kinmel Park Camp.

Sergeant William Dale, passed away while under aesthetic/chloroform while in the hospital at the camp on the 17th March, 1917.

Drummer John P Langford, died 18th June,1917. He was part of the 60th Training Reserve Battalion.

Staff Sergeant Richard Ryan, part of the 59th Training Reserve Battalion, on the 3rd September, 1917. Sadly committed suicide. Yet another life taken by this act at Kinmel Park Camp.

Private Budd, of the 12th Battalion (Home Service) Royal Welsh Fusiliers, aged 47/48, died from TB at Kinmel Park Camp Hospital.

Private Jean Roberts, aged 18, of the Women's Army Auxiliary Corps died in January, 1918. Of Spotted Fever. Her death was questioned by **Mr. Hayden Jones** MP, in the House of Commons, as this young ladies mother was not entitled to a pension. At the time The War Office did not recognize the Queen Mary's Army Auxiliary Corps (QMAAC), serving in their home country.

Lieutenant Arthur Lloyd, aged 29, attached to the Manchester Regiment, was staying at Kinmel Park Camp at the time of his accidental death by fire.

Driver George Brooks, of the Army Service Corps, aged 20, died on the 5th April, 1918. After an accident in Abergele.

Doris Quane of the QMAAC, died 19th April,1918, of an illness. She is buried in St. Margaret's Church, Bodelwyddan.

Private William D Evans, of the Cheshire Battalion (Home Service Battalion) committed suicide in June 1918. By jumping from a moving train.

Private James Gillard of the 53rd, (Young Soldier Battalion) the Welsh Regiment, aged 18, died on the 7th October, 1918. Gillard had contacted acute bronchitis
which he eventually succumbed to.

Private Thomas Dearden, aged 18, of the 53rd (Young Soldier Battalion) Training Reserve Battalion of the Cheshire Regiment, died of influenza, pneumonia and gangrenous appendicitis, on the 14th October,1918.

The following Canadian soldiers died whilst at Kinmel Park Camp:

Sapper 1007062 Albany W, of the 10th Battalion Canadian Railway Troops. He died 10th February, 1919.

Private 3040679 Armstrong G. H, of the 12th Reserve Battalion Canadian Infantry. He died 19th October, 1918.

Private 3111379 Baker H. P, of the 12th Reserve Battalion Canadian Infantry. He died 24th October, 1918.

Private 514556 Baverstock H. P, of the 47th Battalion Canadian Infantry. He died 12th February, 1919.

Gunner 2023376 Bennett G. E, of the Canadian Field Artillery. He died 26th October, 1918.

Private 871099 Bogle W, of the 1st Battalion Canadian Labour Corps. He died 10th February, 1919.

Sapper 636858 Boyce E, of the Canadian Engineers. He died 18th December, 1919.

Lance 781331 Corporal Boyd J, of the 28th Infantry Battalion, He died 15th February, 1919.

Private 5931 Brown G, of the 2nd Battalion Newfoundland Regiment. He died 2nd November, 1918.

Lieutenant Brown R, of the Royal Canadian Engineers . He died 5th September, 1919.

Private 2140485 Cairncross J, of the 1st Reserve Battalion Canadian Infantry. He died 18th October, 1918.

Private 2024695 Card C. R, of the 1st Reserve Battalion Canadian Infantry. He died 20 October, 1918.

Private 901061 Caudle M. H, of the 17th Reserve Battalion Canadian Infantry. He died 22nd October, 1918.

Sergeant 516027 Church A. C .L, of the 1st Siege Battery Canadian Artillery. He died 14th February ,1918.

Driver 3038094 Clarke A, of the Canadian Field Artillery. He died 23rd October, 1918.

Private 3036629 Cleverdon E. N, of the Canadian Reserve Cavalry Regiment. He died 13 February, 1919.

Private 787346 Connell J. A ,of the Canadian Army Service

Corps. He died 22nd February, 1919.

Private 3311772 Cote J, of the Canadian Infantry. He died 22nd February, 1919.

Sapper 164645 Cowan J. A. A, of the 11th Battalion Canadian Railway Troops. He died 27th January, 1919.

Private 2140716 Drips V. P, of the 1st Canadian Infantry. He died 23rd October, 1918.

Private Doel E, of the 12th Reserve Battalion Canadian Infantry. He died 23rd October, 1918.

Gunner 342807 Farrar H. J, of the 2nd Brigade Canadian Garrison Artillery. He died 30th May, 1919.

Private 3312044 Faulkner W. J, of the 12th Reserve Battalion Canadian Infantry. He died 23rd October, 1918.

Sapper 472733 Forbes C, of the 11th Battalion Railway Troops. He died 6th February, 1919.

Private William Frazer, aged 24, a member of the 1st Reserve Battalion Western Ontario Regiment, died on the 24th October, succumbing to illness 'Spanish Flu'. He is buried at St. Margaret's Church, Bodelwyddan. There are many Canadian soldiers buried at St. Margaret's dying of the Spanish Flu.

Gunner 2663566 Garrett G. F, of the Canadian Field Artillery. He died 1st November, 1918.

Private 877467 Gillan D, of the 85th Battalion Canadian Infantry. He died 5th March, 1919. **Killed during the roits.**

Private 103263 Graham O. F, of the Canadian Forestry Corps. He died 26th February, 1919.

Gunner 3059423 Griggs N. J, of the Canadian Field Artillery. He died 27th October,1918.

Gunner 1251417 Haney W.L, of the Canadian Artillery . He died 5th March, 1919. **Killed during the riots.**

Sapper 724241 Henderson J, of the Canadian Railway Troops. He died 27th January, 1919.

Sergeant 282 Jauncey F, of the 11th Battalion Railway Troops. He died 14th February, 1919.

Gunner 338554 Kean G. J, of the Canadian Field Artillery. He died 24th October, 1919.

Private 3232290 Kennedy W. H, of the Canadian Infantry Regimental Depot. He died 6th April, 1919.

Private 3312016 Kent J, of the 12th Reserve Battalion Canadian Infantry. He died 26th October, 1918.

Private 663592 Kerns W. K. A, of the 102nd Battalion Canadian Infantry. He died 9th March, 1919.

Private 4002030 Lapine J. A, of the 4th Reserve Battalion Canadian Infantry. He died 23rd October, 1918.

Private 2184414 Leander R. L, of the Canadian Railway Troops. He died 10th February, 1919.

Gunner 2022937 Lett H. P, of the Canadian Field Artillery. He died 3rd November, 1918.

Private 2140717 Lewis E, of the 1st Reserve Battalion Canadian Infantry. He died 20th October, 1918.

Private 3312087 Loshaw R. J, of the 12th Reserve Battalion Canadian Infantry. He died 24th October, 1918.

Private 3311505 Lynn P, of the 8th Reserve Battalion Canadian Infantry. He died 23rd October, 1918.

Private 666250 Martin A. J, of the 25th Company Canadian Forestry Corps. He died 28th February, 1919.

Private 868230 Martin R .G, of the Canadian Forestry Corps. He died 12th February, 1919.

Private 2023739 Matheson A, of the 1st Reserve Battalion Canadian Infantry. He died 19th February, 1919.

Private 3353035 Meyers F, of the 15th Reserve Battalion Canadian Infantry. He died 18th October, 1918.

Gunner 2650847 Miller L.J, of the Canadian Field Artillery. He died 22nd December, 1918.

Private 725004 Milliken W. B, of the Canadian Forestry Corps. He died 28th February, 1919.

Gunner 342637 Moody S, of the Canadian Field Hospital. He died 17th October, 1918.

Nursing Sister Macintosh R, of the Canadian Army Medical Corps (9th General Hospital). She died 7th March, 1919.

Note: I have written a short story of events involving Nursing Sister McIntosh, earlier in this book.

Sapper 2024860 McCaskill W. F, of the 1st Reserve Battalion Canadian Infantry. He died 24 October, 1918.

Sergeant 114086 McCluskie J, of the Canadian Reserve Cavalry Regiment. He died 27th March, 1918.

Private 2020154 McInnis F. L, of the 1st Reserve Battalion Canadian Infantry. He died 18th October, 1918.

Gunner 336290 McLean C, of the Canadian Field Artillery. He died 19th October, 1918.

Private 763075 McLean W. A, of the Canadian Forestry . He died 17th March, 1919.

Private 475407 McMahon E. G, Princess Patricia's Light Infantry . He died 29th January, 1919.

Private 2383381 Neville A, of the 11th Reserve Battalion Canadian Infantry. He died 5th February, 1919.

Gunner 399200 Park T. A, of the Canadian Field Artillery. He died 23 October, 1918.

Private 2020573 Parsons E. G, of the 1st Reserve Battalion Canadian Infantry. He died 26th October, 1918.

Sapper 913011 Paulson S, of the 2nd Battalion Canadian Engineers. He died 26th October, 1918.
.

Private 249385 Phelps J. S, of the Canadian Army Medical Corps. He died 10th February, 1919.

Private 3162556 Proulx A, of the 10th Reserve Battalion Canadian. He died 30th October, 1918.

Private 436142 Roberts H. G, of the 21st Reserve Battalion Canadian Infantry. He died 30th October, 1918.

Private 2250586 Sands I, of the Canadian Forestry Corps. He died 29th March, 1919.

Sapper 490597 Smith A. G, of the 11th Battalion Canadian Railway Troops. He died 25th October, 1918.

Private 3314639 Stow W. H, of the 8th Reserve Battalion Canadian Infantry. He died 20th October, 1918.

Private 285364 Sumsion F, of the 12th Reserve Battalion Canadian Infantry. He died 8th February, 1919.

Sapper 1057297 Tsarevich W, of the 4th Battalion of the Canadian Railway Troops. He died 5th March, 1919. **He was the Lead Rioter, killed during the roits**.

Sapper 639181 Towsley J. H, of the 11th Battalion the Canadian Railway Troops. He died 30th January, 1919.

Private 2433407 Vaughan D, of the Canadian Forestry Corps. He died 14th March, 1919.

Private 2140613 Waddell J, 1st Reserve Battalion Canadian Infantry. He died 23rd October, 1918.

Private 739739 Walker F, of the 12th Battalion Canadian Infantry. He died 26th October, 1918.

Private 3312094 Wells A. E, of the 12th Battalion Canadian Infantry. He died 26th January, 1919.

Sergeant 436661 White G. S, of the 15thBattalion Canadian Infantry. He died 26th October, 1918.

Gunner 202304 Wilkinson H. G, of the Canadian Field Artillery Brigade Reserve. He died 2nd November, 1918.

Private 766311 Wilkinson W, of the 4th Reserve Battalion Canadian Infantry. He died 6th February, 1919.

Private 3355406 Winters R, of the 15th Battalion Canadian Infantry. He died 2nd February, 1919.

Private 2188525 Wood E. J ,of the 15th Battalion Canadian Infantry. He died 8th January, 1919.

Private 3131221 Wood W, of the 4th Reserve Battalion Canadian Infantry. He died 23rd October, 1918.

Corporal 154059 Woods H. C, of the Canadian Railway Troops. He died 13th February, 1919.

Private 2355366 Wright A. L, of the 4th Reserve Battalion Canadian Infantry. He died 26th October, 1918.

Corporal 438680 Young , of the 52nd Battalion Canadian Infantry. He died 5th March, 1919. **Killed during the riots.**

Private 3214692 Young T. G, of the 21st Battalion Canadian Infantry. He died 23rd November, 1918.

Most of the above named, succumbed to 'Spanish Flu'. Five men were killed in the Kinmel Park Riots. They were **Private Gillan, Gunner's Haney** and **Hickman** whom were shot (Hickman accidently). **Sapper Tarasevitch** and **Corporal Young** being bayoneted on the 5th March, 1919.

Above: The head stone was laid for Private 2188525

Ernest J. Wood, of the 1st Canadian Mounted Rifles, by his brother who served overseas in World War One in the Canadian Royal Engineers (67)

The following 'British Soldier's' died whilst at Kinmel Park Camp

Private 62631 Armstrong G. H, of the Royal Welsh Fusiliers. He died 31st of December, 1916.

Corporal WR/2000559 Beer J, of the Royal Engineers. He died 18th February, 1919.

Lance Bombardier 14100186 Brassington S, of the Royal Artillery. He died 23rd August, 1947. (**Note:** A soldier of the Second World War)

Private 32568 Budd W, of the Royal Welsh Fusiliers. He died 5th September, 1917.

Private 44240 Cleaver A, of the Welsh Regiment. He died 14th June, 1916.

Corporal 36413 Davies R. T, of the Pembroke Yeomanry. He died 5th November, 1918.

Major 15234 Fawcett C. H, of the Royal Artillery. He died 28th November, 1944. **(Note**: A soldier of the Second World War).

Private 9906 Fisher E, of the Welsh Regiment. He died 27th June, 1918.

Private Fenton Harry, of the Manchester Regiment. He died 18th October, 1918.

Private 83763 Greaves C. H ,of the Cheshire Regiment. He died 2nd September, 1919.

Private 59578 Hanscombe P, of the Welsh Regiment . He died 13th April, 1917.

Private 26768 Hext W, of the Training Reserve Battalion. He died 15th March, 1917.

Private TR/3/110218 Jacques F, of the Manchester Regiment. He died 27th October, 1918.

Driver 59314 Jarret P, of the Royal Field Artillery. He died 12th October, 1918.

Pioneer 328580 Johnson A, of the Royal Engineers. He died 3rd November, 1918.

Private 1810 Jones E. N, of the Cheshire Yeomanry. He died 7th June, 1917.

Private 2976 Jones John A, of the Royal Welsh Fusiliers . He died 29th September, 1915.

Private 4/8959 Jones M, of the Training Reserve Battalion. He died 13th March, 1917.

Private 63635 Kay T, of the Royal Welsh Fusiliers. He died 18th January, 1917.

Private 4/80333 Longman G.B, of the Welsh Regiment. He died 13th November, 1918.

Second Lieutenant Martin A. W, of the Welsh Regiment. He died 14th March, 1917.

Private TR/44152371 Noble W, of the Cheshire Regiment. He died 5th July, 1918.

Lance Sergeant 13575 Nuttall J. L, of the Welsh Regiment. He died 25th June, 1916.

Private 82514 O'Conner J. A, of The Kings Liverpool Regiment. He died 21st December, 1918.

Private 78005 Owen G, of the Royal Welsh Fusiliers. He died 13th April, 1918.

Private 87205 Prosser G. E, of the Royal Welsh Fusiliers. He died 25th June, 1918.

Hospital Worker 10515 Quane D, of the Queen Mary's Army Auxiliary Corps. She died 19th April, 1919.

Staff Sergeant A/1615 Ryan R, of the Army Ordnance Corps. He died 3rd September, 1917.

Private 67866 Sheppard W. J, of the South Wales Borderers. He died 30th September, 1918.

Private 4/8720 Simpson L, of the Training Reserve Battalion. He died 3rd March, 1917.

Private 63870 Sutton J. H, of the Royal Welsh Fusiliers. He died 13th January, 1917.

Private 39774 Thompson J, of the Royal Welsh Fusiliers. He died 13th May, 1917.

Lance Corporal D/4588 Townend A. P, of the 2nd Dragoon Guards (The Queens Bays). He died 1st August, 1917.

Private 693 Williams R. H, of the Royal Welsh Fusiliers. He died 2nd November, 1918.

Private 78420 John Sydney Buxton, of the 53rd (Young Soldiers) Battalion the Welsh Regiment. He died 21st October, 1918. He was 18 years of age.

Private TR/4/79924 Fred Ashness, of the 53rd (Young Soldiers) Battalion the Welsh Regiment. He died on the 13th October, 1918, aged 18.

Private TR/4/80369 William Ryder, of the 53rd (Young Soldiers) Battalion the Welsh Regiment. He died on the 12th November, 1918.

Above: The head Stone of Private William Ryder who died of the Spanish Flu, the day after the Armistice. (68)

The last three entries Buxton, Ashness and Ryder all died due to the Spanish Flu epidemic and were taken from the Kinmel Park Camp. They were buried in their home towns with full military honours. In the case of Ashness and Ryder, these men were buried in the Holy Trinity Church Yard in Hurdsfield, Macclesfield, just yards apart. It is believed they were boyhood friends. They joined the Army together, and died more or less together. Quite unbelievable! Buxton is buried at Oyster Mouth Cemetery, Mumbles, near Swansea in S. Wales. I wonder how many more young men died of the Spanish Flu at Kinmel Park Camp, which sadly I could not trace?

'We Will Remember Them'

Finally, I think you the reader would agree this untitled, unclaimed poem is perhaps the most apt of all.

When war is proclaimed and the
Danger nigh
God and our Soldiers is the people's cry
But when peace is proclaimed and all
Things righted
God is forgotten and the soldier slighted.
Even youths grow tired and weary
And young men stumble and fall: but,
Those who's hope in the Lord will

Renew their Strength.
They will soar on wings like eagles,
They will run and not grow weary,
They will walk and not be faint.

Anonymous

This book has taken me many years of researching and collating. Traveling here there and everywhere to get a story. I hope that I have done those who served and continue to serve at Kinmel Park Camp something special to read. The author of the story of **Kinmel Park Military Training Camp 1914-18 (Robert H. Griffiths)** stated, his book was a labour of love. I can concur with his sentiments entirely. I to have tried my utmost to find names of individuals who had a story to be told. Tears were shed, believe me.

Post Script: I truly hope that one day the Union, Canadian and Welsh flags be raised above the graves a **St. Margaret's Church** in **Bodelwyddan** as a permanent tribute to those brave men and women who served and died at Kinmel Park Camp over the past 100 years.

I have carried the torch thus far in the wake of Messer's **Griffiths** and **Putkowski**. It is now up to some other historians, hopefully, to take our work further, regarding Kinmel Park Camp.

John D Johnson

Printed in Great Britain
by Amazon